DEVILS, MONSTERS and NIGHTMARES

DEVILS, MONSTERS and NIGHTMARES

An Introduction to the Grotesque and Fantastic in Art

by HOWARD DANIEL

ABELARD-SCHUMAN
London   New York   Toronto

For John and Leycester

PRINTED IN THE UNITED STATES BY GANIS AND HARRIS, NEW YORK

Contents

Acknowledgments

The author wishes to acknowledge his special indebtedness to the following publishers for the use of copyright material:

Alfred A. Knopf, Inc., New York, for the quotations from *The Social History of Art* (Vol. 1) by A. Hauser, copyright 1951, and from *Cultural History of the Modern Age* by Egon Friedell, copyright 1953.

Oxford University Press, Inc., New York, for the quotations from *The New Testament Doctrine of the Last Things* by H. A. Guy, copyright 1948, and from *The God of the Witches* by Margaret Murray, copyright 1952.

Pantheon Books, Inc., New York, for the quotations from *The Hero with a Thousand Faces* by Joseph Campbell, copyright 1949, and from *The Psychology of Art* by André Malraux, copyright 1949.

Princeton University Press, Princeton, New Jersey, for the quotations from *Goya's Caprichos* by J. López-Rey, copyright 1953.

Holt, Rinehart & Winston, Inc., New York, for the quotation from *The Forgotten Language* by Erich Fromm, copyright 1951.

Charles Scribner's Sons, New York, for the quotation from *Witchcraft in England* by Christina Hole, copyright 1947.

Yale University Press, New Haven, Connecticut, for the quotation from *Psychoanalysis and Religion* by Erich Fromm, copyright 1950.

List of Illustrations

157 GOLTZIUS: *The Dragon and the Comrades of Cadmus.* Engraving. (London, British Museum. Photo Freeman.)

158 BOSCH: *Monsters.* Detail from central panel of *Temptation of St. Anthony.* (Lisbon, National Museum.)

159 *Unicorn Seal from Mohenjo-daro.* (Photo Government of Pakistan.)

160 G. MOREAU: *Oedipus and the Sphinx.* (New York, Metropolitan Museum of Art. Photo Metropolitan Museum.)

161 *Gryphon.* (Paris, Louvre. Photo French Embassy Press and Information Service.)

162 *Gryphon Demon Fighting a Demon.* Cylinder seal. (New York, Pierpont Morgan Library. Photo Pierpont Morgan Library.)

163 *Garuda and Companion.* Indonesia. (Photo Government of Indonesia.)

164 *Pazuzu, the Demon of the Southeast Wind.* Bronze figure. (Paris, Louvre. Photo Archives Photographiques.)

165 CARAVAGGIO: *Head of Medusa.* (Florence, Uffizi. Photo Alinari.)

166 RUBENS: *Head of Medusa.* (Vienna, Art History Museum. Photo Wolfrum.)

167 *Seven-headed Dragon of the Apocalypse.* Illuminated manuscript. (New York, Pierpont Morgan Library. Photo Pierpont Morgan Library.)

168 WORKSHOP OF NICOLAS BATAILLE: Panel from the *Apocalypse Tapestry.* (Angers. Photo French Embassy Press and Information Division, New York.)

169 *Sun in the Zodiacal Sign of the Lion.* Miniature. (New York, Pierpont Morgan Library. Photo Pierpont Morgan Library.)

170 *The 28 Constellations.* Scroll painting on paper. (New York, Metropolitan Museum of Art. Photo Metropolitan Museum.)

171 *Bes.* Faience figure. (New York, Metropolitan Museum of Art. Photo Metropolitan Museum.)

172 CRANACH: *Dwarfs Attacking Hercules.* (Dresden, Picture Gallery.)

173 CRANACH: *Hercules Attacking Dwarfs..* (Dresden, Picture Gallery.)

174 *Monsters* from Herold's *Heydenweldt,* 1554. (Photo Warburg Institute, London.)

175 *Headless Monsters* from Aldrovandi's *Monstrorum Historia,* 1642. (Photo Warburg Institute, London.)

176 *The Sciapod* from Schedel's *Liber Cronicarum,* 1493. (Photo Warburg Institute, London.)

177 *Martikhora* from Topsell's *Historie of Four-footed beasts,* 1607. (Photo, Warburg Institute, London.)

178 *The Crane Man* from Aldrovandi's *Monstrorum Historia,* 1642. (Photo Warburg Institute, London.)

179 *Mahakala.* Bronze figure. (Author's collection.)

180 *A Great Magician* or *Tibetan Flying Sorcerer.* Bronze figure. (Author's collection.)

181 *A Great Magician* or *Tibetan Flying Sorcerer.* Bronze figure. (Author's collection.)

182 *A Great Magician* or *Tibetan Flying Sorcerer.* Bronze figure. (Author's collection.)

183 *Yamantaka and His Shakti.* Bronze figure. (Author's collection.)

184 *Yama—Lord of the Underworld.* Bronze figure. (Author's collection.)

185 *Lha-mo, the Glorious Goddess.* Bronze figure. (Author's collection.)

186 *Citapati, Lords of the Graveyard.* Bronze figures. (New York, American Museum of Natural History. Photo AMNH.)

187 *The Emaciated or Fasting Buddha.* (Lahore, Central Museum. Photo Government of Pakistan.)

188 *Death's Head Jar from Valley of Guatemala.* (New York, Heye Foundation. Photo Museum of the American Indian.)

189 MATHIS GOTHART-NEITHART (GRÜNEWALD): *Pair of Lovers.* (Strasbourg, Musée de la Ville.)

Introduction

"DEAD ARE ALL THE GODS," SAID NIETZSCHE'S ZARATHUSTRA. BUT today the disinterring of these dead gods is almost an industry, for the psychologists and myth-analysts will not let them stay dead. The intellectual Burkes and Hares have been selling the cadavers of the dead gods in the cultural marketplaces of the twentieth century. Hence this book, which largely deals with one of the disinterred, the Devil, with his works and his nightmare realm of sleeping reason.

The scope of this book is that neglected aspect of the subject matter of art which it is customary to call grotesque and fantastic. The definition in the *Oxford English Dictionary* is adequate and helpful for our purposes. To define grotesque and fantastic, it turns to two great English writers, Edmund Burke and John Ruskin; and, of the many meanings of these words, theirs touch most closely on the subject matter of this book. Writing in 1756, Burke had this to say: "All the designs I have chanced to meet of the temptations of St. Anthony were rather a sort of odd, wild grotesques, than anything capable of producing a serious passion." While we cannot now accept his judgment of the emotional content and impact of such works, we are dealing with the same subject matter.

Exactly one hundred years later, Ruskin wrote in his *Modern Painters*: "A fine grotesque is the expression in a moment, by a series of symbols thrown together in bold and fearless connection, of truths which it would have taken a long time to express in any verbal way." As a further refinement, the *Oxford English Dictionary* quotes the *Pall Mall Gazette* of 1888 as authority for its understanding that the grotesque is a branch of the fantastic. The *Oxford* and other dictionaries define the fantastic as being devised by extravagant, wild, and unrestrained fancy, bizarre, whimsical, unreal, and irrational. The works of art which we cover in this book have some or all of these characteristics. But, aside from these pointers, we will not begin with a comprehensive definition of the grotesque and fantastic. That is rather the objective of this book than its premise.

A dualistic approach to life, not altogether surprisingly, has characterized man, that creature with two ears, two eyes, two legs, two arms, and a paired brain, not to mention paired odds and ends of viscera. For such a creature the world very readily falls into a dualism of opposites. He is ever ready to detect a dichotomy in the world of ideas and things: first it was light and darkness, then good and evil, God and the Devil, and, often with disastrous results, white and black. Lately he has been very much concerned with Libido and Thanatos. For good and sufficient reason, the writing of histories of art and culture has been devoted almost exclusively to the works of light and to the greater glory of the Lord; at any rate it has been approached with that purpose. The Prince of Darkness and his ways have been painted, drawn, and carved. But before the immediately recent past it would not have been thought decent to devote any study to the subject. Western civilization needed the Devil and his works too badly to pry into them.

The Devil no longer has functional usefulness, at least not in his old form. Tastes and times have changed. Psychologists at long last have grappled with their real task, the nature and quality of the human soul. They have made some progress towards explaining human behavior. Against this background, and with our ever-ranging interests seeking new and sensational subjects, we can now both profitably and properly see what the Dark Force has inspired in the fine arts.

Before we proceed further, let it be clearly understood that the Devil is dead even if his works are very much alive. This may be an exhumation, but no attempt will be made to breathe life into that numb and pallid corpse which defeated the combined efforts of the Holy Fathers of Decadence, Pétrus Borel, Charles Baudelaire, J. K. Huysmans, Félicien Rops, Villiers de L'Isle-Adam, and Barbey d'Aurevilly, and of their stickier and more epicene English imitators, Swinburne, Beardsley, and the other exquisites of decay. In an appropriate place we will show a few works inspired by these sad and weary souls, but our objective is far wider in scope, if lacking the musty lavender scent of that era. So much for what this book is not about.

In the past several decades, changes in taste and values have made it possible to look a little more dispassionately at the grotesque and fantastic. Previously this would not have been regarded as proper; when value judgments stemmed from the Neo-platonic aesthetics which largely dominated our thinking about art, it would have been outside the pale. Often the apparent and frequently real origins of the grotesque—in the murky depths of the unconscious and the irrational—made it unfit for consumption except by the insulated professions of couch and cloth. But all this has changed now that the lower depths of man's soul have been charted more clearly. Recently, too, Western chauvinism, which used to permit us the indulgence of an occasional gargoyle on our cathedrals, has had to retreat and allow the art of primitive peoples to come out of the dusty halls of ethnology.

This introduction will be as brief as possible. It seems only proper that in a book on grotesque and fantastic art the pictures should speak for themselves. However, as the book is not written for the historian of art and culture, or for the iconographer, it has been thought helpful to add some explanatory notes. Though the pictures in this book, no matter how grotesque or fantastic, are all related to life and to real people, to their dreams, their fears, their desires, and their beliefs, they employ the arcane language of symbols. Moreover, subjects such as the Last Judgment, Hell, and the Temptation of St. Anthony, which loomed large in the mind and comprehension of medieval and early Renaissance man, are scarcely understood or even recognized today. Similarly, although witch-hunting is a familiar aspect of Western man's way of life in the middle of the twentieth century, the quarry and the institution in the fifteenth, sixteenth, and seventeenth centuries were quite different from what they are today. All art may be functional in the broadest sense; but many of the objects illustrated in this book served functions in cultures which are not familiar to most of us. For that reason also it will be necessary to devote some attention in this introduction to cultural background.

A note of warning: It should never be thought that even the most weird, grotesque, and fantastic of the art works illustrated here were considered such by the contemporaries of the artists who produced them. That is entirely our own sophisticated and arrogant view. Ungrounded as we are in the customs and ways of life of the cultures which produced them, our eye examines them and our brain relates what it records to its own frame of reference.

The human eye and man's imagination have always been fascinated by the bizarre and the unusual. The urge to create grotesque and fantastic art is as old as art itself. Down through the ages artists have put as much energy into creating and depicting the fantastic—devils, monsters, and nightmares—as they have put into the production of works filled with the trappings of recognizable reality. The late Henri Focillon saw life as a permanent organism in which all forms of the past were capable of survival. He pointed out that "the life of the fantastic in art ebbs and flows throughout time—an indestructible strength and source of inspiration."

The grotesque and the fantastic have always been popular. This is borne out by the frequent appearance of these subjects in the graphic arts, the media consciously chosen by the artist in order to make his work available to a large audience. What we choose to regard as bizarre—the devils and hellfire of the Bosch-Brueghel underground—was understandable and important in the emotional life of the common people in the early sixteenth century. Notwithstanding the emergence of a middle class with the rise of capitalism and the development of the Protestant Reformation (a middle class with a supposedly rational frame of reference, broadened and enlightened by the great discoveries in physics, astronomy, and geography), there still exists a vast public for the visually startling and bizarre.

Today's curiosity about the grotesque and fantastic has been considerably stimulated by the rediscovery of such geniuses as Bosch, Brueghel, Callot, and Goya. But this curiosity has only been stimulated; by no means has it been satisfied. Later we will hazard a few guesses as to why the mind of our times finds this subject matter so engrossing. For the present we note that the historians of art have concentrated, understandably enough, on those aspects of the fine arts which are not fantastic and are, superficially at least, quite rational. Though there is an obvious justification for this emphasis, particularly in view of our inherited tradition of classic and idealistic beauty, it has resulted in glossing over the devotion poured out by many great artists on the fantastic and on the related subjects which exist beyond the pale.

We have already said that this is a book which deals largely with the Devil and his works. As the Devil can live the good life only in a religious world, this is also a religious book; for it does deal with a central problem of all religions, the problem of how man's soul fares during his residence here on earth. Man, his soul quavering in the presence of the unknown, within or without, reacts in one of two ways. He uses reason in trying to master the strange world in which he finds himself; or, if he is much given to terror, he bows down abjectly before forces which he regards as all-powerful, relentless, and unknowable. However, as he must occasionally come out into the world of sunshine, he uses the remnants of his ability to rationalize and persuades himself that these forces can be propitiated. He then labors hard to build up an incredibly complicated system for dealing with these propitiable forces. But, whether our artist is a man of reason or of unreason, his reaction to the unknown is the source and stimulus of all the grotesque and fantastic works illustrated in this book. For their creators have dropped their buckets into the deep, dark wells of the unknown and have brought up into the light of day these devils, monsters, and nightmares.

It is rare to find an artist who is entirely rational in his approach to the dark forces; and the artist who unconditionally surrenders to the unknown is equally rare. It is a long way from the rationalist humanism of Brueghel, Callot, Goya, and Daumier to the unknown artists who modeled the funeral urns of certain pre-Columbian civilizations, or who carved the ferocious New Guinea and West African masks. A vast number of artists fill the space and time between the extremes. They are divided by an imaginary line which separates those who attempt to explain the unknown by reason from those who abandon reason and resort to other defenses against the werewolves.

The men of reason may have their occasional lapses. This is understandable, for they are dealing with the darker side of man. But in directing the light of reason into this darkness they rout the monsters whose dwelling place it is. They can say, with Goya: "Imagination, deserted by reason, begets impossible monsters. United with reason, she is the mother of all the arts, and the source of their wonders." Also, like Goya, they can show that these monsters are ridiculous. But because of the hold that these night terrors, hobgoblins, and demons have on the popular imagination, they make good use of them as symbols in attacking the folly and wickedness in which man wallows when he is against himself. Whether it is a *Capricho* of Goya or the *Uli figure* from central New Ireland, each of the works collected in this "museum without walls"—to borrow Malraux's wonderful phrase—was produced by an artist, known or unknown, who concerned himself with those forces in man which, if uncontrolled by reason, would destroy him.

It is no accident that in the second half of the twentieth century grotesque and fantastic art has aroused enormous interest. We are witnessing an outburst of latter-day romanticism, of which in many ways this interest is an aspect. This movement, which arose out of the ferment producing the French Revolution, signaled the breakup of the old social, economic, and political structure. It released prodigious quantities of energy, which burst through the ancient obstructions. Out of it emerged and developed that unfettered intuition, imagination, and fantasy of northern Europe which we contrast with the classicism, reason, order, and harmoniousness of the Mediterranean south. In our time we are no longer tossed and torn in the strife between these two ways of interpreting in artistic terms the meaning of life. Our fevered generation has for the first time fallen heir to the culture of the whole world. But, as Malraux points out, we are part of an "agnostic civilization," unoriented, not knowing where we are going, not caring, or pretending to be indifferent. We are now on a great eclectic binge in which it is every man for himself. The simple cry out for some humanistic rationalist to show them not only where they have been, but where they are going.

No longer are we forced to weigh the merit of art works solely in the scales of our

Western heritage. As Malraux has so eloquently shown, the revision of art values which began in the nineteenth century wiped out the prejudice against what was regarded as clumsy art. Until that time all art was measured by Italian standards. Masters as great as Rubens and Velázquez were admired for the wrong reasons, for the Italianism which was read into them. Gothic art was disdained; its creators were thought to have failed or been unable to copy classic sculpture. And even today the prejudice in favor of the so-called Mediterranean tradition lingers on. The art works of cultures as diverse as those of Tibet and Arnhem Land are ordinarily hidden away in museums of natural history. But photography has contributed greatly to freeing us from these bonds and opening up for us that wider world of art foreseen by Baudelaire as early as 1860, when he extolled the beauty of pre-Columbian, Euphrates, and Nile Valley arts.

The revision of art values was itself the result of other changes. A vast revolution in man's knowledge, psychological awareness, and sensibilities has been going on during the last fifty years. Modern psychologists have shown us how to penetrate deep into man and his hidden world. Consciously or unconsciously, to paraphrase Reik, we now examine grotesque and fantastic art with the "third eye," for the unconscious has its reasons which reason knows nothing of. Indeed, many of us have been overstimulated. Having cracked the hard nut of form for form's sake and found little nourishment inside, we now march bravely under the banner of Freud in search of the richer diet of inner meaning which lurks beneath the artistic exterior of grotesque and fantastic art. But psychology is far too important a subject to leave to the psychologists. Thanks to the pioneer work of Freud and others, it has found its real subject, the shape and quality of man's soul. The discoveries of the pioneers have been immensely useful to the poets and creative artists, and thus their indirect contribution to grotesque and fantastic art has been considerable.

Widespread literacy and the enormous expansion of the mass media have opened up cultural vistas never before dreamed of. The demand for new material is almost insatiable. David Riesman has shown how the controllers of the mass media, always on the hunt for fresh material, are too busy with the mechanics of their media to have time to create or find this new material themselves. Instead, they pursue the *avant-garde* as relentlessly as the Eumenides pursued Orestes—but not punitively, merely to plunder it of its fads, fancies, and discoveries. And part of this plunder is grotesque and fantastic art. For this art and its creators have been a source of interest and fascination to the *avant-garde* for almost a generation. Never has there been such interest in artists like Bosch, Brueghel, Goya, and Ensor, to mention a few—and in the surrealists, too, who have made their contribution through the publicity given them by the mass media. The furor caused by this publicity alerted the mass media to the entertainment possibilities of grotesque and fantastic art. But let it not be thought that Bosch, Brueghel and these others are surrealist; notwithstanding the parentage wished on them by the proper surrealists, intent as any bastard to prove themselves sprung from honorable loins, they are anything but. All of these artists, so long the property of the *avant-garde*, have been taken over by the mass-culture media. Great magazines now run color spreads of their works, accompanied by entertainingly written articles making them understandable to a larger and larger audience. The *avant-garde*, in perpetual flight from what it considers vulgarization, is discovering or rediscovering newer, more fantastic, more grotesque, and more obscure artists.

The wild, violent elements in grotesque and fantastic art are well suited to today's taste and to the temper of the times. Only art works which hit with a fearful wallop make much of an impression in the fierce competitive atmosphere of this age. So this art appeals to an ever-growing public for some of the reasons that have enabled psychotic, perverted whodunits, stuffed with murder, snobbery, and violence, to reach an enormous audience.

These are troubled times: in spite of great material gains, contemporary man is scarcely delirious with happiness. Certainly there is enough evidence of the malaise of the Western man's soul. The psychoanalysts and other students of society tell us that this disease has been eating at our vitals since World War I. Indeed, some of them have told us this so loudly and so long that it is almost bad form not to be convinced of it. Occasionally we begin to suspect that these "eager pessimists," to use Karl Kraus's famous phrase, are part of the disease they purport to cure. Howbeit, there can be no denying that man today is rarely at peace with himself and the world. Is it any wonder that he escapes from his worries into the world of sleep and dreams? This has been graphically put by Fromm:

> Modern man is exposed to an almost unceasing "noise," the noise of the radio, television, headlines, advertising, the movies, most of which do not enlighten our minds but stultify them. We are exposed to rationalizing lies which masquerade as truth, to plain nonsense which masquerades as common sense, or as the higher wisdom of the specialist, of double talk, intellectual laziness, or dishonesty which speaks in the name of "horror" or "realism," as the case may be. We feel superior to the superstitions of former generations and so-called primitive cultures, and we are constantly hammered at by the very same kind of superstitious beliefs that set themselves up as the latest discoveries of science. Is it surprising, then, that to be awake is not exclusively a blessing but also a curse?

If, then, man finds the world of sleep and dreams attractive, it is not hard to see why he is drawn to works of grotesque and fantastic art which bear more than a superficial resemblance to that world.

The material available on the grotesque and fantastic is bewilderingly abundant. But it is readily available only to the scholar and the specialist in the unorthodox. As this book is to serve as a rough chart to guide the traveler across this terra incognita, it will limit itself to pointing out the general topography and will not produce a definitive map with all the blank spots filled in. As the title indicates, this is an introduction. And so we make no effort to cover the whole field of the grotesque and the fantastic. Neither will we cover all the art works illustrating our main topics. To do so would be repetitious, and there would be little profit or entertainment in it.

This collection of some of the better-known monsters produced by mankind in the visual arts during the past five thousand years gives special prominence to the Devil, the master of sleeping reason. We will sketch the portrait of the elusive one and his helpers, examine and count his staff, explore his home, watch him at work, and look in on his friends the witches. We will then make a brief excursion into the world of monsters, real and imaginary. Finally we will survey the terrain of sleep and probe some of the dark caverns of the dream and the nightmare.

Well may we wonder at the disparateness of the strange subjects illustrated in this book. But there is a link which binds all of these subjects together. Man is that link; for man facing up to the unknown has produced all of them. And they all have in them, to a greater or lesser degree, the essence of Goya's dictum that the sleep of reason produces monsters. Without doubt there is much matter for wonder here. But wonder, as Socrates tells us, is the beginning of wisdom.

Devils

THE DEVIL IS THE WORLD'S OLDEST CITIZEN. HE WAS BORN LIKE A flash of lightning in some remote past when the first human being was seized with unspeakable terror of the unknown. Since then he has thrived mightily in that vast baggage of terror which mankind has subsequently dragged along with it through life. For the Devil is nothing more than the symbol of man's fear of the unknown. In man's mind he is the personification of darkness, unreason, the power of destruction, malevolence, and the absence of love; and attributed to him is that magic which Voltaire called the secret of doing what nature cannot do. As the learned editors of the *Encyclopaedia of the Social Sciences* point out, "the conception of a malevolent power is probably of greater antiquity and stronger potency than the idea of a beneficent deity; for fear has been considered the first incentive of religious worship and propitiation of evil powers regarded as the first phase of all religious ceremonies."

PROFILE OF SATAN

The figure of the Devil, familiar in many guises to the Western world, first emerges clearly in the post exilic literature of the Jews. The apocryphal writings of Enoch, that early traveler through Heaven and Hell, are a prime source of information on Satan and his cohorts. But the Jews cannot be blamed for creating the Devil; for that gentleman, later to acquire considerable education and charm, and a high polish to his well-rounded personality, has always had universal citizenship: in the Moslem world as Satan, in the Zoroastrian world as Ahriman, in China as *t'an-mo*, among the Manichaeans as the Demon, and among the Tantric Buddhists as Mara.

In his most primitive aspect Satan is the symbol of physical evil, that force in nature which causes natural disasters like floods, famine, disease, earthquakes, and solar eclipses. The development of the other, subtler Satan, the master of moral evil, comes much later and is of considerably more interest. Our concern is with both Satans, for his representation in art ranges from the crude but terrifying fetishes of primitive peoples to Delacroix's sophisticated portrait of Mephistopheles in his illustrations for the first part of Goethe's *Faust* (Fig. 1).

Let us look at the Devil as a young man, as he was when he and God were indistinguishable to all but the initiated. The original Jehovah of the earlier parts of the Old Testament was an omnipotent but harsh and inexorable Lord, quite lacking in Christian charity. He united in himself both God and Satan, for, speaking through Isaiah, he could say, "I form the light, and create darkness; I make peace, and create evil: I, the Lord, do all these things." The development among the Jews of a subtler moral system suggested the advantages of a more equitable division of labor between God and Satan. The forcible dissolution of the partnership inspired some of Dante's and Milton's most stirring lines. And so eventually we find Satan doing business under his own firm name.

It is interesting to learn that the Greeks and Romans, whose pantheons were quite crowded, never found place for one single personification of evil. Some of their gods, like the Roman Saturnus, did evil things, but it was only part-time activity. True, Baldung-Grien's *Saturnus* (Fig. 2) looks capable of infinite wickedness, and Goya's picture of Saturnus eating one of his children (Fig. 3) is ghastly; but this is avocation, not profession. In the keenly competitive religious atmosphere of the Mediterranean, Judaism, and later Christianity, derived considerable advantage from limiting the occupants of their pantheon to one. At the same time there is reason to doubt whether they benefited by infinitely magnifying the population of Hell. But this division of labor did make God more kindly and godlike, and the Devil more utterly wicked and even satanic.

Hindu iconography has some gory figures but, as Germain Bazin has pointed out, few figures which can be described as demonic; the Bali hell-hound of our illustration is more theatrical than demonic (Fig. 4). With the great subtlety developed during centuries of intense study of the nature of the world, Brahmanism, in what Bazin regards as one of the boldest metaphysical efforts ever made, tried "to resolve the external dualism in one grandiose myth—the myth of the terrible *Siva*, both god and devil, mystic lover and seeker after blood, obsessed by the will to destroy and yet frantic to create: a cosmic myth which raises evil from the level of appearance to a level of transcendental reality at which it becomes transformed into the highest good" (Fig. 5).

In the history of civilization, the ultimate neap tide of sleeping reason seems to have washed the shores of the pre-Columbian Aztecs. This was followed by a spring tide of diabolism, which expressed itself in torrents of ever-replenished blood. This civilization, in which the citizens expected the end of the world every fifty-two years, shivered in an atmosphere so impregnated with terror that death must indeed have been a happy release.

The Devil has been an absolute necessity for the Christian Church. If the early Christians had not been fortunate enough to have on hand the Jewish Satan, they would have been forced to create a substitute. One most noticeable characteristic of the early Christians was their obstinate non-objectivity where their religion was concerned. In the protection of their interests the early (and some of the later) Christians could match the zeal of a twentieth-century cartel. The intensity of their devotion to monotheism was such that all other gods immediately became monsters of the direst iniquity. This attitude added depth, complexity, and amazing versatility to the character of Satan. The loss of the charm and beauty of such gods as Diana, Venus, Apollo, Mercury, Neptune, and Vulcan, who were consigned to the deepest depths of Satan's abode, cannot be gainsaid. At the same time they certainly added glamour to sin. With the fall of the Roman Empire the character and mien of Satan were immeasurably broadened by the recruitment to his side of all the gods and devils of the pagans.

With the passing of time the face of the Prince of Darkness has become uglier and more monstrous, like the picture of Dorian Gray. Being incorporeal and pure spirit, he has learned much from the wiles of Proteus. He assumes different guises for different purposes. In the days of the early church fathers, when the Greeks' distaste for what they regarded as the ugly was influential, Satan was pictured as a handsome young man. Later Christians showed their revulsion for this too subtle idea by mutilating the face of this good-looking Satan. It was this sanctimonious attitude which was responsible for the partial destruction of a section of the St. Gregory Nazianzen manuscript in the Bibliothèque Nationale. Beginning with Romanesque art we have nothing but monsters.

This protean quality of Satan has made it difficult to bring his likeness into sharp focus. Then, too, the Church frowned upon a straight and simple portrait of Satan. He could be shown only in his most frightening and temporary guises, as when he was at work on some overtaxed soul. It is this common, or garden, devil who appears in work clothes in Duccio's *Temptation of Christ* (Fig. 6) and in St. Theresa's life, with his "hideous" form, "horrible" mouth, and "terrible" voice. As from some space rocket, there proceeds from his body "a great flame, perfectly bright without any shadow." The pig's face of the Accursed One—a not uncommon form assumed by him in Germany—can be seen lurking behind the stern Christian knight in Dürer's engraving *Knight, Death, and Devil* (Fig. 7).

After the sixteenth century's great and pathological fever of satanism and witchcraft had abated itself, the subject went into a long somnolence. Since then Satan has fitfully wakened in recognizable form only a few times in the fine arts. He shows up in full regalia in a few English romantics like Fuseli and Blake (Figs. 8 and 9), and watered down and slightly melodramatic in Martin. In the last shudder of romanticism, the decadent movement, he makes his farewell appearance. The enormous expansion of book publishing in nineteenth-century Europe was his chance for a last fling. The works of Huysmans and the other writers of decadence fairly reverberate with the hollow clatter of cloven hoofs. We catch our last fleeting glimpses of him in Rops's powerful etching *Satan Sowing Weeds* (Fig. 10). With the burial in 1947 of Alastair Crowley—the self-styled Great Beast—we can now be reasonably assured that the great god Satan is dead.

THE DEVIL'S STAFF

Man's complete, unmitigated depravity, as seen by Lutherans and Calvinists of the extreme right, suggests logically that there is no further work for the Devil to do. But this view is perhaps exaggerated. There is much work yet to be done. And it has always been thus.

The first well-organized census of the demon kingdom was conducted by some of Luther's students. The results, published in Feyerabend's *Theatrum Diabolum*, reveal that in the middle of the sixteenth century there were 2,665,866,746,664 devils. For information concerning this census, and for many other fascinating facts about the public and private life of the Devil, we owe much to his witty biographer, the ironic Italian scholar Arturo Graf. Delving into the records, he unearthed a contemporary and more eager demonographer who estimated the devil population at ten thousand billion! It is possible to suspect exaggeration here. A moderate and more reasonable estimate was made a few years later by Dr. Johann Weier. In his *De Prestigiis Daemonum*, published at Basel in 1568, he released some of his findings. If we assume that there was no hidden unemployment, and if we allow for seasonal factors, we obtain a picture of a full-employment economy. We learn that the Adversary's kingdom has 72 princes and 7,405,926 devils, divided into 1,111 legions, each consisting of 6,666 devils. Weier is careful to note that his figures may be subject to "errors of calculation"; this is understandable, for he did not have the magic tools of the modern census-taker. This sixteenth-century Paul Bunyan then goes on to classify devils as igneous, aerial, terrestrial, aquatic, subterranean, and lucifugous. (A more detailed classification would have called for the talents of a metaphysical Linnaeus!) At the same time, notwithstanding these wild imaginative flights, Johann Weier was one of the first men to take a firm and courageous stand against witch-hunting. Such a paradox was not infrequent in an age when magic was turning into science.

The early Church fathers believed that devils had bodies of incredible lightness, not much denser than air or fire. To nourish such bodies, it was said, they dined, rather unsubstantially, off the smoke of pagan altar-fires. But they were also reputed to have quite a palate for blood.

The appearance of devils, especially those of the working class, presents no problem at all. A whole host of artists and sculptors have provided posterity with most accurate portraits of thousands of them. Of course, the ability of devils to assume different shapes, many of them the monstrous offspring of miscegenations between species of the animal, plant, and mineral kingdoms, so brilliantly recorded by Baltrušaitis, must have kept the artists on the run. But the main varieties—some of which are illustrated in this book—can be seen very clearly, warts, scales, horns and all, in the works of Lochner, Signorelli, Urs Graf, Bosch, Grünewald, Brueghel, and Rubens (Figs. 11–19). These artists, well versed in the writings of the demonographers, have done a pretty thorough job of covering the demon kingdom.

With the Renaissance recovery of certain Greek attitudes towards the beautiful, demons, in the work of such Neo-platonic painters as Michelangelo, graduate from the horrible to the awesome (Fig. 20).

Some of the guises assumed by demons must certainly have enlivened medieval evenings, for, according to the chronicles, the bedchambers and even the beds of virtuous ladies like Queen Kunegund were infested with devils disguised as beautiful young men. As we can see in our illustrations, demons were also much given to obscene exposure and other forms of exhibitionism. The medieval evening of even the most blasé soul would have been shattered by some of the scatological carryings-on of these demons.

THE DEVIL AT HOME—HELL

Even if our demonographer statisticians were only ten percent off in their calculations, it is only too apparent that the task of moving one's residence on earth to permanent quarters in Hell presented few problems. The short, flying visit was another matter, however, though whatever the difficulties here, many succeeded in solving them. It seems that the task never attracted those with a passion for anonymity. There is an extensive list of the names (often with addresses) of visitors to Hell, starting with Ulysses and coming up through time to Aeneas, Enoch, St. Paul, St. Guthlac, and Huon of Auvergne, to mention but a few. As is to be expected, the early Irish, those great travelers, were well represented by St. Fursey and the wicked knight Tondale. This last traveler's account of his short vacation from life, *Visio Tondalis*, was one of the best-known pieces of literature in the late Middle Ages. His journey, like those of most of the others, was well known to the greatest of the voyagers to darkness, Dante.

The accounts brought back by these travelers were tremendously popular and were a part of most people's everyday fund of knowledge until several centuries ago. They are the authority for many of the works illustrated in this book.

From our illustrations it might be thought that devils were always gadding about and had no home. This suggestion of idleness is not altogether fair, for they were invariably about their master's business, maintaining, among other things, a vast card index of each individual's sins. And they did most definitely have a home. The quality and character of this home varied considerably from one civilization to another, whether it was the Kigallou of the Mesopotamian civilizations; the Court of Osiris of the Egyptians, where the infernal hippopotamus consumed the souls of the guilty; the Douzakh of the Zoroastrians; the Naraka of the Hindus; the Hel of the Nordic world; al-Hotama of the Moslems; the Sheol of the ancient Hebrews; the Gehenna of the New Testament; the Hades of the Greeks; or the Hell of Western Christendom. Once again the Jews were responsible for a colorful concept which has added much to our life, especially to the latter part of it. It is amazing that a local belief of a numerically small people could have entered so strongly and durably into the system of ideas of millions. For "Gehenna" is the Greek form of the Hebrew phrase for "Vale of Hinnom." This desolate ravine outside Jerusalem was used as a dump for city refuse. The garbage had been burning for many years, and the smell and dismal appearance of the place had even been commented on by Christ.

Virtually all civilizations have conceived a place for the dead. The special Christian contribution to this aspect of metaphysics has been Hell as a place of punishment, populated by hyperthyroid devils. Not far removed from this concept are the Brahmanic and Buddhist hells, the latter extraordinarily complex with its 136 regions; but these have a much more temporary character than the Christian hell, for, at best, they are way stations interrupting the long journey of the soul's transmigration.

It is surprising that there is a general lack of agreement concerning the whereabouts of a place which is the destined home of a substantial part of humankind. It has been variously located in the Far East, the Far West, and the Antipodes, at both the north and the south pole, under most European volcanoes which are still active, under distant islands in unknown seas, and even under lovely County Donegal, Ireland. The descriptions of most visitors to darkness would locate Hell anywhere from a few feet beneath the earth's surface to the very center of the globe. The same lack of agreement arises concerning the shape, size, and location of the portals of Hell. One form of entrance which appears very frequently is the dragon's or monster's mouth. This can be seen in the works of Bosch and Brueghel (Figs. 21–23) as well as in many illuminated manuscripts. The number of these entrances is uncertain, although the well-intentioned Enoch states emphatically that there are but three, each of them guarded by serpent-like creatures, "their faces like lamps that are gone out, their eyes like darkened flames, and their teeth naked down to their breasts." Dante's famous gate is best remembered for the slogan engraved above it: "Leave all hope, ye that enter."

The size, topography, and, indeed, everything else concerning Hell have been described with such inconsistency that one is reminded of characters in a Pirandello play, each seeing a situation which would never be recognized by the others. This applies not only to size and topography, but also to economic geography, climate, and flora and fauna.

Estimates of the size of Hell vary considerably. Cornelius a Lapide calculated in the seventeenth century that its area was about 40,000 square miles, or somewhat smaller than the State of New York or the German Democratic Republic. Even if such demongrapher statisticians were only approximately right, and we disregard the enormous hordes of sinners, truly unconscionable overcrowding would have resulted in such a confined area. Evidence of overcrowding can be seen in works by Thierry Bouts, P. Christopsen, Memling, the Limbourg brothers, Fries, and Brueghel (Figs. 24–30). It would seem more reasonable to follow Enoch, who estimated Hell as 216,000 times larger than the earth. Allowing for the much smaller size of the earth in those days, this would make it considerably larger than the State of Texas.

Enoch, Dante, and other distinguished travelers describe Hell as being divided into seven compartments. The Italian is quite precise on this score, and everyone is familiar with the neat, geometrically arranged circles whose circumferences get smaller the nearer we get to the center of the earth. The descriptions of the topography vary from Enoch's bottomless flaming abyss, sixty times hotter than fire, to Tondale's and Dante's descriptions of vast expanses of landscape and substantial urban development, most of it permanently afire. According to the Manichaeans, the landscape is "cut up by deep gulfs, abysses, pits, quagmires, dikes, fens, and pools, into expanses of land divided and split up by long stretches filled with thick forest interspersed with vents which . . . send up a smoky exhalation; while afar off . . . arise columns of fire and smoky cloud." Many of these accounts vividly describe ugly plants covered with razor-sharp thorns and poisonous fruit. And the weather would break the heart of an aneroid barometer; for, simultaneously, the visitor is likely to experience the burning sirocco, a blizzard with heavy hail, frost, and sleet, torrential rain, earthquakes, thunder, lightning, showers of red-hot meteorites, and ever the suffocating fumes of smoldering sulfur. All of this is found copiously illustrated in the works of Bosch and Brueghel. But the interest of these two artists in the form, texture, and atmosphere of the underworld landscape is quite unlike that of any subsequent landscapists. For there was a deep didactic under-current in all their work. Thus the *Hell* in Bosch's triptychs *The Hay Wagon* (Fig. 31) and *The Garden of Earthly Delights*, or *The Millennium* (Fig. 32) is bursting with satire and social criticism. And so too is Brueghel's *Dulle Griete*, with its castigation of the hyperthyroid, shrewish woman (Fig. 33). As an illustration, the German scholar Fraenger has shown that the group of figures with musical instruments in *The Millennium* (Fig. 34) is a satire on the new polyphonic church music recently introduced into the Netherlands by Josquin des Prés and Jean d'Okeghem.

After these two painter-geniuses, Bosch and Brueghel, finished with the subject of Hell, there was nothing further to be said about it in the visual arts—at least nothing serious. Later artists who tried their hand, like Callot, were entertaining, but in purely theatrical terms (Fig. 35).

The excessive development of the idea of terrible punishment by hellfire, to keep people on the straight and narrow path of rectitude, gave too many hostages to un-reason. The dawn of the modern scientific world provided a more suitable climate for the incomparably harder task of building into human nature a behavior machine which runs on reason. Hell, as Sartre has shown, we still have with us, but it is no longer external; it is Milton's "which way I fly is hell, myself am hell."

THE DEVIL AT WORK—TEMPTATION

Devils at work have provided the subject matter for some of the wildest flights into the realms of fantasy ever made by artists of the Western world. They are dealing with a subject which has infinite possibilities and which, judging from the fervor and heat of the attacks on sin, is more than passably attractive to most of us. But temptation and its inevitable follower, sin, did not spring fully developed from the head of Satan. The concept was thoroughly worked out and completely matured in Asian philosophy more than two thousand years ago. Since then, with a few notable exceptions, it has been largely debased and lost in a myriad of details. Philosophy's loss has been art history's gain, for this subject has exercised and tested the quality and scope of imagination of such artists as Sassetta, Bosch, Patinir, Schöngauer, Cranach, Brueghel, Huys, Grüne-wald, Parentino, Callot, Teniers the Younger, Ensor, and even, today, Ernst and Dali (Figs. 36–60).

The most glorious recorded story of temptation is that relating the trials to which Gautama was subjected before attaining enlightenment and becoming the Buddha. We will give a somewhat detailed account of some of these trials, for this incident in the life of Buddha is an archetype of the temptation story.

The legend states that the future Buddha had just sat down under the Bo Tree when he was attacked by Mara, who sought to break his concentration. This would distract him from his devotion and so prevent him from attaining enlightenment. The Devil used every weapon in his armory, including his three voluptuous daughters, Desire, Pining, and Lust, but to no avail. It should be remarked that when the Devil is working on figures of divine proportion like Gautama, he uses the temptations of the flesh as an opening gambit, well knowing that he will lose his pawns. This gesture is the tribute he pays to tradition. Only when he is working on lower-case mortals do the temptations of the flesh become pawns in a winning move.

The story continues that Mara moved all his most powerful pieces and then gave the signal to attack to his fearful army.

This army had the power to take on all manner of different appearances, transforming itself endlessly in a hundred million ways. Its body and hands and feet were wrapped in the coils of a hundred thousand serpents, and in its hands were swords, bows, arrows, pikes, axes, mallets, rockets, pestles, sticks, chains, clubs, discuses, and all other instruments of war. Its body was protected by excellent breast-plates. Its heads and hands and feet turned in all directions. Its eyes and faces were flaming; its stomachs, feet and hands of all shapes. Its faces glittered in terrible splendour; its faces and teeth were of all shapes, its dog-teeth enormous, fearful to behold. Its tongues were as rough as mats of hair, its eyes red and glittering, like those of the black serpent full of venom. Some were spitting the venom of serpents, and some, having taken the venom in their hands, were eating it. Some, like the garudas, having drawn out of the sea human flesh and blood, feet, hands, heads, livers, entrails and bones, were eating them. Some had bodies of flame, livid, black, bluish, red yellow; some had misshapen eyes, as hollow as empty wells, inflamed, gouged or squinting; some had eyes that were contorted, glittering, out of shape; some were carrying burning mountains, approaching majestically, mounted on other burning mountains. Some, having torn up trees by their roots, were rushing towards the Bodhisattva. Some had the ears of stags, pigs, elephants—hanging ears or boars' ears. Some had no ears at all. Some, with stomachs like mountains and withered bodies made from a mass of skeleton bones, had broken noses; others had stomachs like rounded jars, feet like the feet of cranes, with skin and flesh and blood all dried up, and their ears and noses, their hands and feet, their eyes and heads all lopped off. . . .

Some with the skin of oxen, asses, boars, ichneumons, stags, rams, beetles, cats, apes, wolves, and jackals, were spitting snake venom, and—swallowing balls of fire, breathing flame, sending down a rain of brass and molten iron, calling up black clouds, bringing black night and making a great noise—were running towards the Bodhisattva. . . .

This account from Chinese sources is illustrated almost literally by the Tang dynasty painting from the Caves of the Thousand Buddhas at Tun-huang, painted in the tenth century of the Christian era (Figs. 61–63).

The story goes on that during all of this hubbub the future Buddha remained unmoved. He then touched the earth with his fingers, and Mara's hosts disappeared. At daybreak the following morning Gautama achieved complete enlightenment.

Almost eight hundred years later we find the Devil using identical tactics against an equally worthy opponent, Anthony of Egypt (A.D. 250–350), and with equally little success. Whether the Devil was in a rut or the early Christians were made of incredibly rugged material, we shall never know.

Anthony came of wealthy parents. At the age of twenty he heard a church sermon admonishing the congregation to sell their goods, give the proceeds to the poor, and follow Christ. With one of those sudden decisions which are common in the lives of the great, Anthony there and then unburdened himself of his wealth and headed for the wilderness. He established himself near Fayum in the Egyptian desert, as the first hermit. Notwithstanding the rigors of open-air life (some of the more fanciful rigors will be described shortly), he thrived, living until he was more than a hundred years old. During this long and desiccated existence he created a monastery for the other hermits who had answered the call of the desert, taking time out but once to assist in the extermination of the Arian heretics.

We have as authority for the deeds of Anthony no less a light than the great St. Athanasius. His life of St. Anthony is the source for the glowing story in Jacobus de Voragine's *Golden Legend*. The account of the temptations which follows uses the translation made and published by William Caxton in 1483.

He had overcome many temptations of the devil. Then on a time when he had overcome the spirit of fornication . . . the devil came to him in the form of a little child all black, and fell down at his feet and confessed that he was the devil of fornication, which St. Anthony had desired and prayed to see . . . to know him that so tempted young people. Then said St. Anthony: since I have perceived that thou art so foul a thing I shall never doubt thee.

After, he went into a hole or cave to hide him, and anon he found there a great multitude of devils, that so much beat him that his servant bore him upon his shoulders into his house as he had been dead. When the other hermits were assembled and wept his death, and would have done his service, suddenly St. Anthony revived and made his servants to bear him into the pit again where the devils had so evil beaten him, and began to summon the devils again, which had beaten him, to battles. And anon they came in form of divers beasts wild and savage, of whom that one howled, another sniffled, and another cried, and another brayed and assailed St. Anthony, that one with the horns, the others with their teeth, and the others with their paws and ongles [claws], and disturbed, and all-to rent his body that he supposed well to die. Then came a clear brightness, and all the beasts fled away.

Had the Devil the wit of Oscar Wilde, one wonders what havoc he might not have wreaked among the holy hermits infesting the Egyptian desert. A Wilde story, as good as it is apocryphal, relates that the Devil once spied a swarm of imps worrying a holy man, who paid no attention to them. Calling off his apprentices, he told them to watch how an expert worked. Changing himself into a young hermit, he walked over to the holy man and whispered in his ear that the hermit's brother had just been appointed Bishop of Alexandria. Immediately an angry scowl came over the holy man's face.

It is understandable that the Christian West, with its exaggerated concept of the role of sin in human affairs, should have devoted attention to classsifying sins into an orderly system. By a combined process of refinement and distillation this was achieved in the extra-Biblical idea of the Seven Deadly Sins. The authority for this neat, convenient, and portable set of sins was not holy scripture but the bravery and concentration of holy fathers working with explosive material. The standardization which has now come down to us is in great measure the work of St. Thomas Aquinas, who based himself on the work of St. John Climacus, St. Gregory the Great, and earlier church fathers. The Seven Deadly Sins, according to the great author of the *Summa*, are pride (*superbia*), covetousness (*avaritia*), lust (*luxuria*), envy (*invidia*), gluttony (*gula*), wrath (*ira*), and sloth (*accidia*). Those who might wonder that pride and envy are included would do well to remember that these are the sins which led to the eviction of Lucifer from Paradise. Such sins are appropriate to devils, who, being incorporeal, cannot themselves participate in what the ignorant might consider to be more interesting pastimes. This is a Thomist conception. There are other schools of thought, equally convinced that devils bar no sins, interesting or uninteresting. These and the other sins can be seen in particularly interesting form in the painting by Bosch, in the engravings after Brueghel, in the charming etching of Callot, and in the engraving of Posada (Figs. 64–68).

THE DEVIL AS MASTER OF DESTRUCTION

Such are the aggressive forces lurking beneath the hide of man that it has generally been found easier to be destructive than creative. This is a ready-made situation for the Devil, who is the master of destruction. In this area he is uncontested commander, in both the retail and the wholesale field, which we will now examine. Our survey will deal with but two aspects of the Devil's destructive handiwork. First we will see the Devil at work channeling the destructive energies of man into such disgraces as torture and martyrdom and into other shameful displays of violence. And then we will look at some works illustrating that most shameful, destructive, cruel, and irrational of all man's activities—war.

This survey will be purposely brief. Artists have devoted far too much attention to these subjects, particularly to martyrdom. We have an embarrassing quantity of such works, but, with the exception of several major subjects such as the Crucifixion, they are deficient in inspiration. Most martyrdoms lent themselves better to literary than to pictorial treatment.

Most pictures of martyrdom are run-of-the-mill commissions, and one has the impression that the painters had little stomach for the gorier side of their work. With their own eyes they had seen too much of the barbarous punishments of their day to want to do more than reproduce them literally in their paintings. The subject did not offer the philosophical and aesthetic challenge which they found in Death, Hell, the Last Judgment, and Temptation. In the work of such artists as the unknown sculptor of the School of Amiens, Cranach, Bouts, Lochner, and Liferinxe (Figs. 69–75), we are struck by the sufferings of the martyr and the monstrous quality of the torturers. Our reaction is one of horror rather than of compassion. Quite different is Pisanello's drawing of hanged men (Fig. 76). Here is the dispassionate scientific observer, who jots down just what he observes without any emotion. (On the same sheet he has sketched two other figures, elegant and very much alive.)

With later artists, like Caravaggio, Callot, and Hogarth (Figs. 77–80), we move back from the world stage and watch man's crass inhumanity to man. But we are filled with compassion, not only for the victims but also for the torturers, who are equally, but less painfully, the victims of wickedness.

The subject of war has inspired singularly little great art. Great works have been created on this subject, but their greatness lies in what the artist has had to say about it, and not in the grim subject itself. Of the eight artists whose work has been chosen to illustrate this subject, three had really little to say of a social nature concerning war. Pollaiuolo used his *Battle of the Ten Naked Men* as an exercise in drawing, particularly of nude bodies (Fig. 81). The violent mayhem being done by the participants is incidental to the artist's concern with his purely technical problem, which he solved by producing one of the best drawings of the nude seen during the entire Renaissance. Bosch, in his odd little detail from the Lisbon *Temptation of St. Anthony*, appears to be concerned only with the fantasy of aerial warfare (Fig. 82), while the anonymous contemporary Balinese artist is interested primarily in the design of his *Hanuman Battling Rawana* (Fig. 83).

The works of Callot and Goya are fraught with social comment. Callot's *Great Miseries of War*—the direct inspiration of Goya's *Disasters of War*—express this sensitive artist's nausea at war and all its horror and futility (Figs. 84–86). He had seen various phases of the Thirty Years' War, including the ravaging by mercenary foot-soldiers of his own beloved Lorraine. For him, as for any rational man, there was no romance or glory in war, and even less in the lives of those who lived by it. The meaningless destructiveness of this life has nowhere been expressed better than by his contemporary Grimmelshausen, the humane author of the immortal *Simplicissimus*.

> For gluttony and drunkenness, hunger and thirst, wenching and dicing and playing, riot and roaring, murdering and being murdered, slaying and being slain, torturing and being tortured, hunting and being hunted, harrying and being harried, robbing and being robbed, frighting and being frighted, causing trouble and suffering trouble, beating and being beaten: in a word, hurting and harming, and in turn being hurt and harmed—this was their whole life.*

Goya, too, felt the horror and futility of war. But there is added intensity in his work, for it is charged with national spirit. It excoriates not only the institution of war but war as an instrument of national policy. For at the time he etched his plates, war could be seen only through the lens of the French invasion and the horrors and calamities it wreaked on the Spanish people (Fig. 87).

This concern with the horror and waste of war is also reflected in the work of Rousseau, Ensor, and Kubin (Figs. 88–90). The macabre humor of Ensor's *Battle of the Golden Spurs* stems from a long Flemish tradition. Kubin's grim work *War* was a frightening anticipation of the relentless destruction that was to come in two world wars.

THE DEVIL'S FINAL TASK—THE LAST JUDGMENT

The day of days for the devil population is the day of the world's end, the Last Judgment, when in Matthew's words, the sheep will be divided from the goats. On this day the souls of both the quick and the dead will be weighed, while entire demondom strains impatiently for the signal to start permanent chastisement of the damned.

The delight of the Romanesque and Gothic periods in pictorial illustration has been commented on by many art historians. That the artists of the period seized on the subject of the Last Judgment with avidity was not fortuitous. Eschatological literature— a frightening name for a frightening subject—had been accumulating for more than a thousand years. Most of it was gloomy, for it reflected the pessimistic times in which it was written. Most people were aware, in a broad sense, of the events which were expected to take place when the world came to an end. And in times of stress they reacted to this gloomy picture in an exaggerated and highly emotional way. During this period eschatology was well nourished by history. For this was an age characterized by a millenary psychosis, a set and nearly universal belief that the end of the world was actually close at hand.

*Grimmelshausen: *Simplicissimus the Vagabond*. Translation by A. J. S. Goodrick (George Routledge & Sons, London).

This age produced excessive virtue and excessive vice. It even produced in Emperor Frederick II a fascinating forerunner of the skeptical, disbelieving modern man. He is the alleged author of the notorious book *De tribus impostoribus*, which developed the thesis that the three greatest deceivers known to history were Moses, Christ, and Mohammed! Not for nothing did one pope call him the Antichrist.

The atmosphere in which medieval man lived was charged with psychological terror and surcharged with the physical horrors of the Black Death, the Jacquerie, the extermination of the Waldenses, and other blood-bespattered examples of man's appalling inhumanity to man, which well justify Friedell's description of it as the "world nightmare."

The Church must certainly have encouraged artists to portray the Last Judgment—if not for didactic purposes, then for political purposes. The obvious lesson was that all human beings, be they kings or serfs, would be judged, and only the Church could intervene to put in a good word for the accused.

The developed concept of the Last Judgment comes from the New Testament. It is true that the first of the writing prophets, Amos, described the Day of Yahweh, when everybody would be judged; and the Book of Daniel has some glowing passages on the dreaded end. The subject found its most devoted supporters in the writers of the Apocrypha: the Book of Enoch, the Book of Jubilees, and the Apocalypse of Baruch. It should be remembered that what in these books seems strange to us, who no longer have time for the small print of holy writ, was common knowledge to most people during the Middle Ages.

The early eschatological writings are often nationalistic, and we sense that the writers are getting even with their national enemies. The principal later development was the internationalization of eschatology. The writ of the Last Judgment now runs everywhere.

There are devotion, detailed care, and, in the case of the northern artists, obvious enthusiasm in the way this climactic scene is represented by the unknown sculptors of the tympani of Bourges and of many other Romanesque and Gothic churches, and by Signorelli, Lochner, Bosch and Huys and their imitators, by Van Leyden, Van Cleve, Brueghel, Michelangelo, Tintoretto, Tom Ring, Martin, and Allston (Figs. 91–104).Their heavy emphasis on the plight of the damned and their vagueness concerning the rewards of the saved suggest the general air of pessimism which pervaded life during those times.

In his study of the end of the world, H. A. Guy, the learned divinity master of a British public school, says that consideration of the hereafter "has come to the forefront in a remarkable manner during the present century." With a commendable excess of professional zeal he has probably exaggerated the conscious interest of the ordinary person in his ultimate fate. But today even the people in Louis MacNeice's poem, who seem to want nothing more than "a bank balance and a bit of skirt in a taxi," have been startled by a few atomic explosions into occasional, hazy consideration of the dreaded end. There has never been such a time for eschatology. Whether the Western religions are satisfying this need goes beyond the scope of this book. However, what does concern us here is the sort of subject matter treated by artists at other times when the arid smell of the hereafter permeated everyday life.

FRIENDS OF THE DEVIL—WITCHES

Witches have always been with us. The whirring of broomsticks, the bubbling of caldrons, and the chattering of covens are always most remarked during or shortly after major economic, political, or social disturbances. Lest we feel arrogant, it is well to remember that Kittredge pointed out, in his apologia for the comparative reasonableness of seventeenth-century New England witch-murderers, that witchcraft in one shape or another is still credited by a majority of the human race. Belief in witches is another of the hostages which sleeping reason gives to irrationality.

The intellectual climate in which artists live is to a greater or lesser extent reflected in their work. When we consider the vast literature on witchcraft widely circulating in western Europe in the fifteenth, sixteenth, and seventeenth centuries, it is surprising that the witch does not appear more frequently in the fine arts. Of course, most art works during that period were commissioned by the Church or by rich patrons whose ideology was basically not different from that of the Church. It is unlikely that such patronage would have called for this kind of subject matter. Except for an occasional *Saul and the Witch of Endor* (Fig. 105), it may be assumed that most of the works which have survived were executed for their creator's pleasure.

The known historical facts are that from the end of the fifteenth to the middle of the seventeenth century western and northern Europe was plagued by the paranoia of witch-hunting, during which bloodthirsty psychotics hounded thousands of innocent victims to a variety of ghastly deaths, of which burning was the most common. How many tens of thousands perished as a result of this madness will never be known. But the many who perished in Geneva in the terrible year 1515, and the twenty thousand death warrants said to have been signed by the Protestant jurist Carpzov, give credence to Raiponce's estimate that there were 50,000 witch executions by burning or otherwise in Germany, Belgium, and France alone, before the madness exhausted itself.

Although this morbid phenomenon appeared all over Europe, its most virulent outbursts took place in northern Europe. Two places which were virtually free from the disease—and Catholic writers have set great store by this—were Ireland and Rome. But much has been made of the Catholic persecution of witches. The papal bull *Summis desiderantes* of Innocent VIII was issued in 1484. It expressed great concern at the large numbers of the faithful in Germany who had forsaken their religion and gone in for hot lusting with devils. To right this unholy situation two ecclesiastical gumshoes named Sprenger and Kramer were forthwith commissioned to extirpate this wickedness. Taking at its face value the injunction in Chapter XXII of the Book of Exodus, "Thou shalt not suffer a witch to live," the two paranoiac Dominicans labored hard. Two years later they produced their infamous *Malleus Maleficarum* (Hammer of Witches), an obscene monument to anti-feminism. Armed with their technical manual, they then proceeded to destroy by frightful tortures hundreds of innocent women.

However, the Protestants were equally zealous; for Calvin and Knox not only instigated witch-burnings and torturings but were actual eyewitnesses. One of John Knox's first actions expressed in Scottish parliamentary legislation was the imposition in 1563 of the death penalty for witchcraft. A practical man about such matters, "that maist notable servant of God," as his first biographer called him, was wont to have them burnt in his very presence. Even crowned heads vied with these holy men, and in 1595 we find James I bursting into print with his *Daemonologie*.

This hysteria brought out the worst in everyone and provided rich manure for the warped growth of the ignorant and the psychotic. It provided an atmosphere—which has since occurred only once—in which the professional witness and denunciator could become the hero of the day. Christina Hole, in her *Witchcraft in England*, provides some interesting information on this occupation:

Many took to this lucrative trade and gained money and reputation by travelling from place to place and profiting by the hysteria of the inhabitants. They came into a district, pronounced their verdict upon the people submitted to them, took their blood money, and went away. The accused were handed to the courts for trial, and if they were subsequently proved innocent, no punishment for false testimony was visited upon the witch-finder.

The very title of the Sprenger-Kramer opus, *Malleus Maleficarum*, hints at the anti-feminist bias of the witch-hunters. The most noticeable characteristic of the disease was a wild and vicious hatred of women. With very few exceptions the hecatombs were made up entirely of women. Anti-feminism has had a long and shameful history. Some of it has been flavored by worthy bishops such as Clodius, who, after careful study, concluded that woman was a bag of manure. This attitude was widespread until well past the Renaissance, and it found its clearest and most popular expression in Jean de Meung's *Roman de la Rose*. Sprenger and Kramer summarized this attitude with a question: "What is woman but a foe to friendship, an unescapable punishment, a necessary evil, a desirable calamity, a natural temptation, a domestic danger, a delectable detriment, an evil of nature in fine colors?'' There can be little doubt of the crying need of the two pitiful authors of this nonsense for spiritual and psychiatric help!

Culture historians, like Friedell, who have been much influenced by the discoveries of psychoanalysis believe that "the problem was not a religious, but a sexual one under religious disguise . . . the result of mass-psychosis due to repressed sexuality, manifesting itself in gynophobia." It was probably a lot more than that; for, as the old and somewhat static world of the Middle Ages broke up and the modern world began to form, the disorders of adjustment produced many other depressing examples of irrationality.

The question whether or not there were witches who engaged in magic and who celebrated some sort of sabbath seems too ridiculous to consider. At a time when belief in witches was universal, the scholars Albertus Magnus, St. Thomas Aquinas, and Duns Scotus were skeptical about their powers, but Nider, the author of the terrible *Formicarius*, was quite convinced of their supernatural authority. It is doubtful whether even psychotic, power-crazed politicians really believe in the existence of witches today; yet the brilliant and persuasive studies of the English anthropologist Margaret Murray seem to have established the existence and survival until fairly recent times of a European witch cult whose rituals included worship of a horned beast. She marshals some weighty evidence to prove that witchcraft was nothing more than the survival of an "old, honorable and obstinate religion dating back to prehistoric times."

The great nineteenth-century French historian Michelet, in his compassionate, if somewhat intuitive, study of satanism and witchcraft, anticipated some of Murray's findings. If we can accept Michelet's grim picture of the physical and mental miseries of the Middle Ages, we can readily understand that the unhappy masses were often driven to despair. Indeed, Michelet puts forward a convincing case for the widespread existence of what was called devil-worship. It would seem that Christianity was only a thin veneer, under which throbbed the hearts of the old pagan devils. It is the recorders of history, with their canonical bias, who have falsified the record. It is not hard to believe that at one time or another the abused serfs of western Europe found little help in Christianity and took their troubles to the old and well-established visitors from darkness. Their credit rating was at least as good as that of the so-called messengers of light. For, unlike the new god, the old gods broke no promises, for they gave none.

Our illustrations provide us with a strange and interesting paradox. The works of the fifteenth- and sixteenth-century artists Bosch, Baldung-Grien, Nikolaus Manuel-Deutsch, and Van Oostsanen, all of whom gave credence in one degree or another to the supernatural powers of witches, are far less satanic and convincing than those of Goya. And yet Goya believed not one whit in their existence or powers. The purpose of his etchings was to show the absurdities which the imagination is capable of producing when the mind is abandoned by reason (Figs. 105–111).

If we think that this problem has been solved once and for all, let us not forget Murray's reminder that much witchcraft still survives today, and that, although the anthropologists are crowding the ships and planes making for Africa, Australia, and the Andes, "the so-called advanced countries offer to the investigator the richest harvest in the world."

FACES OF THE DEVIL—MASKS

The Devil has thousands of faces, and the grotesque character of some of the most terrifying of them has been permanently captured in the art of the mask. By no means all masks are portraits of the Devil, but many are, and it is with these that we are mainly concerned.

The making and wearing of masks has a long history, dating back at least 20,000 years to the last Ice Age. The wall paintings in the caves of south western France and northern Spain frequently show male figures wearing horned animal masks. And so, too, do Egyptian paintings and statues such as the Ptolemaic *Anubis* of our illustration (Fig. 112). The use of masks has been well-nigh universal since then, and there have been very few cultures in which they do not appear in one form or another.

There are many different theories concerning the origin of masks, none of which is completely convincing. We can feel more solid ground under our feet when we deal with the function of masks, the purpose for which they exist. For masks have a very specific function. Among most peoples living in primitive forms of society, the emotion of fear has a full, over-rich life. Such peoples spend a considerable part of their lives coping with fear in its many forms, fear of predatory beasts, of human enemies, of the forces of nature, and, worst of all, of the dark unknown. The mask developed as one of the tools of magic for coping with these fears. Spindern calls it "the instrument par excellence with which to handle supernatural powers." And it was heavy with magic, the most potent part of which insulated the user from the perilous powers he was dealing with. Thus it was felt that the wearer of an animal mask acquired the qualities of the animal depicted by the mask. Similarly, the wearer of a mask representing a god, a practice common in the pre-Columbian civilizations, was thought to acquire some of his powers. Terrifying masks representing destructive demons would neutralize, ward off, or even frighten the enemy. In all probability the Gorgon's head was originally such a mask. A similar purpose can be detected in African masks and pre-Columbian masks in the form of funerary urns (Figs. 113–118). And the author saw in China a few years ago masks put on children in order to scare off the demon of smallpox. Malraux has pointed out that the proper rendezvous of these savage masks is the witches' sabbath; when a collection of them is brought together, we have an *haute couture* of Death.

Masks are used in a variety of social activities, the most notable being the secret society and the ritual dance. In the Duk Duk societies of the Southwest Pacific, the masks portray monstrous beings from the other world who carry off to the unknown those who breach the norms of established social conduct. The masks are said to portray the cassowary, but the only thing they have in common with that seen-to-be-believed bird is utter fantasticality (Figs. 119–123). On a more practical level the terrifying masks are frequently used in secret societies to create a suitable atmosphere for blackmail and extortion. In Tibet or Ceylon they are used to exorcise demons. Among the Iroquois, who were troubled by spirits lacking arms, legs, and bodies, the Ga-Go-Sa, or appropriately named False Faces—a mask-wearing society of men—performed dances to drive off these visitors from darkness. The masks are fantastic and more satiric than terrifying (Fig. 124).

The carry-over of the mask into the more developed societies often has a dramatic emphasis and is also associated with dancing. It is this aspect of the mask which lies behind Frazer's theory of the magical and religious origin of drama. "Actors sought to draw down blessings on the community by mimicking certain powerful superhuman beings and in their assumed character working those beneficent miracles which in the capacity of mere men they would have confessed themselves powerless to effect."

But even with the mask's more sophisticated use in the dance and drama of ancient Greece, Rome, Ceylon, Indonesia, China, and Japan, the face of the demon peers out at us, and we know we are not far from the primitive rituals of exorcism and sympathetic magic (Figs. 125–133). With the masks of the Indians of both the Northwest and the Southwest we are right in them (Figs. 134–140). Indeed, the Indians of the Northwest have reached such heights of sophistication that in certain dance festivals the rich hire the poor to wear the masks which are considered unlucky! Among the Eskimos, masks not only have their magic function but also contain the subtle and unexpected quality of laughter. This indefinable admixture of laughter and terror has been noted by many authorities as characteristic of Eskimo art (Figs. 141–143).

The mask has still some importance in the theater and dance of western Europe. But it has lost much of its ancient inspiration and become alienated from its divine or diabolic roots. By the time we reach the seventeenth and eighteenth centuries the masks in such centuries-old theater as the *commedia dell' arte* have much charm but mighty little of the Devil. The masked figures in Callot's *Balli di Sfessania* are the Devil as clown and not as tempter (Figs. 144 and 145). And in Magnasco's and Tiepolo's delightful *Pulchinellos* they are little more than sad and undernourished strolling players (Figs. 146–148).

Exotic Monsters And Other Fabulous Beasts

Before man emerged from his enchanted world into the modern world of history and disenchantment, he had to rationalize the unknown and the unknowable. It was a day for the unfettered imagination, where only magic was law. And what more obvious way of explaining power in the world than to attribute it to superbeasts, which frequently combined the characteristics and frightening mien of half a dozen denizens of the animal kingdom, including man himself. Certainly a chimera or an eastern-style dragon (Figs. 149–151), vivid in the mind's eye, was more permanently terrifying than a glimpse of a wolf skulking on the outskirts of a forest.

Fashion, that marvelous institution which has enabled each passing generation to feel superior to its predecessor, has moved in a wondrous manner. The subject of monsters and fabulous beasts has had its changing fashions, too. Indeed, there has been a well-defined mode in monsters. The earlier Christians, with their discovery of the only True Way, scorned classical antiquity's zoological garden full of hissing gorgons, soaring Pegasus, snapping hydras, singing sirens, roaring Minotaur, and stamping satyrs (Figs. 152–154). Far more sophisticated to them were the creatures carefully catalogued in their bestiaries; their own basilisk, chimeras, gargoyles, hippogriff, unicorn, wild men, western-style dragons, and salamanders (Figs. 149, 155–157). Very little of this menagerie was of domestic origin. Many of these unshriven horrors had, like lemmings, moved west, probably originating in the arcane infinity of central Asia.

In moving out of completely fantastic Asia, the monsters frequently acquired a more natural and rationalistic appearance. This was due in some measure to the pre-Renaissance influence of Greek thought. A slender evidence of this rational note can be observed in the monsters described in the letter allegedly written by Prester John to the Christian princes of twelfth-century Europe. This spurious document stirred up the embers of the medieval imagination with its fevered descriptions of his fantastic kingdom, peopled by inconceivable monsters ranging from Gog and Magog to salamanders which spun thread with the composite qualities of nylon and heat-resistant tungsten.

In the western Europe of the Middle Ages much of the grotesque decoration of ecclesiastical architecture was directly inspired by the monsters carried in effigy in popular festivals and processions. Thus the stonemasons who carved the gargoyles on churches in the Ile de France were thoroughly familiar with the legend of the great dragon Gargouille, which ravaged the Seine and neighboring areas until sent forth to another sphere by the trusty weapon of the gallant St. Romain of Rouen. Effigies of Gargouille, of chimeras and like monsters, were a feature of both religious and secular processions for centuries. Many of these monsters are more appropriately dealt with elsewhere in this book. At this point it suffices to note the detail from Bosch's Lisbon *Temptation of St. Anthony*, with its summation of medieval monsters (Fig. 158).

UNICORN

The first inhabitant of our garden of fantastic zoology is the unicorn (Fig. 156). This noble beast of Indian lineage made a decorous entry into Europe by way of the ordinarily restrained *Natural History* of Pliny. What was good enough for Pliny was certainly good enough for the Middle Ages and the Renaissance. The unicorn became very upper-class and fashionable, for it was believed that scrapings from its horn were a sure antidote for poison. They were also claimed to put fire into old men's blood. All of this fairy story has some slight connection with the real world. A confusion on the part of scholars translating the Old Testament into Greek gave the unicorn even greater respectability and certainly more glamour than a rhinoceros could ever expect to achieve without outside help. For undoubtedly it is the rhinoceros which was converted into the unicorn.

In passing, it is worth noting that each age produces its skeptics. St. Bernard excoriated the monks who busied themselves painting and drawing the unicorn and other strange beasts: "What business have those . . . marvelously beautiful freaks . . . in front of the eyes of the monks who are supposed to be reading or meditating?"

While we may sympathize with St. Bernard's concern at the monks' neglect of their spiritual exercises, what they lost in reading and meditating was our gain in a great treasury of beautiful, if sometimes startling, illuminated manuscripts.

In its passage through the literatures of many cultures the unicorn swelled into a monster so large that no accommodation could be found for it in the Ark. Imaginative chroniclers of the Middle Ages report that throughout the entire period of the Flood it swam the troubled waters tethered to the gunwales of the Ark. Such was the inflammation of man's fancy that when early Western travelers such as Marco Polo actually saw a rhinoceros, they would not accept that ugly beast as a unicorn. And, as our five-thousand-year-old seal from Mohenjo-daro suggests, beasts even stranger than the rhinoceros roamed Asia (Fig. 159).

The gentler side of the Christian storytellers accounts for the most charming quality of the unicorn. Young ladies of unimpeachable virginity alone could tame it. Without casting any shadow on the purity of medieval womanhood, we can only assume that the taming process melted the unicorn's bones into butter. For no unicorn bones or other relics have so far been discovered.

SPHINX

The next strange creature in our tour through the mythological zoo is the Sphinx. This lion's body with a human head emerged from the wasteland of the Middle East some five thousand years ago and has haunted man's imagination ever since. Our specimen, as Gustave Moreau makes only too clear in his now somewhat strained flutter at viciousness, is the deadly female of the Greek species (Fig. 160). This strange lady is generally equipped with wings and a nasty disposition. According to legend, she was altogether unsporting in her attitude towards visitors to Thebes who failed to answer correctly her simple question, "What animal goes on four legs in the morning, two at noon, and three in the evening?" Failure to give the correct reply, "man," put her in a terrible tantrum. This inevitably resulted in the traveler being thrown off a high cliff, into a ravine. The embarrassment to the city fathers of Thebes, concerned about the good name and fame of their town, must have been considerable. The timely arrival of

Oedipus, who answered her riddle correctly, put an end to her game, and she joined her victims by throwing herself into the ravine. Oedipus was rewarded for his cleverness with the throne of Thebes. He had already unknowingly killed his father. He then proceeded, equally unknowingly, to marry his mother, bringing all manner of trouble on everyone, particularly himself.

There are many versions of the Oedipus story. Writers and scholars have understandably selected the one which supports their own pet theory. It is stimulating and encouraging, to those who fear that the fire in man's imagination is dying down, to see what an intelligent man can do with a suitable version of a good myth.

As early as the seventeenth century we find Topsell putting forward a rational explanation of the myth. In his version a scorned and deserted Queen of Thebes named Sphinx made off with her unloving spouse's treasure, got together some husky henchmen, and proceeded to interfere with the free trade and commerce of Thebes. This kind of freebootery was known in the Theban language as an "enigma." The price put on the head of Sphinx and her "enigma" attracted the doughty hero Oedipus, who with the powerful argument of his sword solved the problem for the ungentlemanly King of Thebes.

Then we have the equally sensible but more penetrating and scholarly nineteenth-century version of J. J. Bachofen. His great contribution to the study of myths, noted by Fromm and others, was to show that the kernel of the story contains "cherished memories of the past." The version chosen by Bachofen is signally uninterested in erotic overtones or undertones, and the sphinx is merely background. The real issue, according to Bachofen, is the struggle between the dying matriarchal system and the fast-emerging patriarchal system. The punishment of Oedipus is meted out for killing his father, even though unwittingly, and not for incest with his mother.

Finally, in the twentieth century, we have such figures as Freud choosing the generally known version which we have just related. Freud used it to give brilliant and exotic color to his theory of the Oedipus complex, with its ailments and disorders which can develop in the infant who senses a rival for the love of his parent of opposite sex.

GRYPHON

Another of the strange and exotic hybrids which roamed the Middle Eastern imagination was that shocker known variously as the gryphon, griffon, or griffin. A lion's body topped by the wings, claws, and sometimes the head of an outsize eagle, he came in different sizes and styles, from a miniature model with alert, pointed ears to a giant whose flight could temporarily obscure the sun (Fig. 161). Cylinder seals from the Tigris-Euphrates civilizations, such as the one illustrated, also show a gryphon variant, an eagle's head and wings mounted on a muscular human body. He is generally called a gryphon demon (Fig. 162).

From the gryphon's representation in art he seems to have spent a considerable part of his time exchanging knife thrusts with other ferocious and utterly imaginary beasts in a struggle for scrawny pieces of livestock. His startling appearance and inclination for lethal weapons must surely have endeared him to the hearts of men in many warlike civilizations.

If he could be said to have any gainful occupation, it was that of guardian of the gold and treasure of the East. A less spectacular activity engaged in by gryphons was guarding the dead. Indeed, as the gryphon moved west, he seems to have been put to work at more practical tasks, such as pulling the chariots of Zeus and Nemesis.

Hybrids, especially if they are as imaginative in conception as the gryphon, have always exercised a fascination over man's imagination. And so we find the gryphon represented in art all the way from Peking to Paris. For the Western world his incorporation into the trappings of heraldry has secured him permanence. Without him, Gothic heraldry, which that great scholar Focillon called a "museum of Romanesque monsters," would lack one of its most interesting specimens.

GARUDA

A not too distant relative of the gryphon is the garuda, a combination eagle-man. The garuda in our illustration comes from Indonesia (Fig. 163). The native habitat of the man-bird is that part of Asia which thrilled to the derring-do of the *Ramayana* and the *Mahabharata*. It is described in the latter treasure-trove of myths as "the bird of life . . . destroyer of all, creator of all." Of course, a similar tag has been put on half a dozen other players in the *Mahabharata*. We must always make allowances for the enthusiasm of copy-writers and myth-weavers. The garuda is said to be one of the earliest creations of man's imagination and is probably attributable to his search for an explanation of the sky. A relative of the garuda is Pazuzu, the Babylonian demon of the southeast, or fever, wind (Fig. 164).

The principal activity of the garuda is the killing of snakes. This worthy undertaking has been completely successful in one country only, and there probably because his assistant was an Irishman.

A symbol of victory, the garuda has been immortalized in the surface decoration of the great architectural monuments of Southeast Asia, particularly Angkor Wat and

Borobudur. Today he continues to be seen in the state symbols of several countries of Southeast Asia and, quite appropriately, as the symbol of an Indonesian airline.

MEDUSA

The medusa is another creature which can be convincingly interpreted according as we see little to laugh at in the world and follow the unromantic myth-analysts, or as we have a sense of humor and follow the romantic zoologist Willy Ley. Indeed, this writing on monsters is greatly indebted to that vastly entertaining writer.

What is significant to those who take their myths straight is that the lovely Medusa, one of the three Gorgon sisters, had a torrid love affair with Poseidon the sea god. The course of true love never running smooth, not even for Greek royalty, their impatient passion one day found fevered satisfaction in a temple of Pallas Athena. This frustrated and premature feminist, who did not like Poseidon anyway, got off her bile on poor Medusa. She transformed that beauty into a repulsive woman with writhing snakes for hair. One look at this monstrosity would turn the viewer to stone. Not satisfied with her handiwork, the soured Athena then provided Perseus with some special equipment which enabled him to slash off the unfortunate woman's head without suffering any ill effects himself. The severed but still writhing head is the subject of startling paintings by Caravaggio and Rubens (Figs. 165 and 166).

Approaching this monster from seaward, Willy Ley shows that the ancients were merely using their imaginations to explain the giant octopus. This sea monster, better known in more recent times as the kraken, was just as terrifying to the ancients as to us. Indeed, Homer, in the twelfth book of the *Odyssey*, describes graphically Odysseus' meeting with one of this brood, in business under the name of Scylla. Ley leaves little doubt that Medusa-Scylla is a symbolic representation of the giant octopus.

BEASTS IN THE BOOK OF REVELATION

The philosophical ideas which are the concern of the Apocalypse, or Book of Revelation, are dealt with in another place. Here we pause to identify one or two of the more lurid freaks which troubled the midnight calm of medieval man and, even in this age of apparent enlightenment, provide round-the-clock alarm for Christians of Fundamentalist persuasion.

Though the animal symbols of sin in the Apocalypse are presented in fascinating garb, they can hardly be said to be attractive. For all the monsters in the Apocalypse

garb, they can hardly be said to be attractive. For all the monsters in the Apocalypse are representations of Satan, and it would never do to show the Whore of Babylon as the well-built, good-looking girl she probably was. Some of the Apocalyptic beasts probably knew better days, when they could fight it out with formidable heroes on a beast-to-man basis, without being troubled by idealogical issues. The seven-headed dragon in our illustration is fully occupied in vomiting up evil spirits and would probably not be recognized by the Hydra, his nine-headed ancestor, who haunted the Lernean Marshes until done in by the dauntless Hercules (Fig. 167). That these monsters appealed to the imagination of medieval man is evident from their appearance in illuminated manuscripts, from the ninth to the fifteenth century, and in the glorious fourteenth-century tapestries now in Angers, known as the *Apocalypse Tapestry* (Fig. 168).

MONSTERS OF ASTROLOGY

In earlier civilizations astronomy and astrology were inextricably intertwined. The forerunners of science often made sharp and accurate observations of heavenly phenomena. But their rudimentary science was ill served by artists with a predilection for the monsters of unreason and with little if any interest in natural phenomena. The picturesque and largely anthropomorphized aspects of astrology appealed to the artist. Thus an Indian miniature painting of the Mogul period shows the Sun in the zodiacal sign of the Lion as a divine figure riding on the back of a lion (Fig. 169). These zodiacal signs are frequently painted in the so-called "animal style" of the steppes, in which the main figure is constructed ingeniously from dozens of tiny figures of animals and human beings.

There were virtually as many systems of astronomy and astrology, both closely related to divination, as there were civilizations. Some of these zodiacal systems, such as the Indian, and particularly the Chinese, were incredibly complicated (Fig. 170). One is continuously amazed that more work was not put into the less strenuous activity of straight ratiocination. The millennia before Oscar Wilde seem to have been crowded with hopeful people who believed that Nature imitates Art.

It was not until the Renaissance that we find artists like Dürer concerned not only with the symbolic animals and figures of the zodiac but also with the natural phenomena of which they are a fascinating reflection.

DWARFS AND PYGMIES

Since the beginnings of recorded history the dwarf has been a popular figure in painting and sculpture. In Egypt as far back as 3000 B.C. we find sculptors of the Old Kingdom carving his likeness with considerable accuracy. They also carved the likeness of pygmies and showed clearly their awareness of the pathological differences which distinguished dwarfs from those other undersized people.

It was the Pharaohs who started the odd custom of having dwarfs as a part of the royal entourage. Dwarfs were also highly prized by the dance-loving Egyptians for their skill in that art. One of the most interesting human documents we have from ancient Egypt is a letter written in the Sixth Dynasty by the youthful Pharaoh Neferkare. He expresses his anticipation and excitement at the prospect of receiving a present of "a dwarf of divine·dances from the Land of the Spirits," who will "dance the divine dances to cheer the heart of the King of Upper and Lower Egypt."

A certain prestige was attached to dwarfdom; we even find some dwarfs graduating from the courts of royalty into the Egyptian pantheon—namely, Bes, the god of war (Fig. 171), and Ptah-Sohar, the god of fire.

In northern European mythology and folklore dwarfs are often closely associated with magic. As elves and goblins they lived deep in the heart of the mountains, where they guarded rich ore bodies unknown to all mortals except Wagnerians who had steeped themselves in the *Ring of the Nibelungs*. This earthy species, which appears in Cranach (Figs. 172 and 173), contrasts with the gentlemanly types who appear in the paintings of Rubens and Velázquez.

MARVELS OF THE EAST

In the brief foray into teratology, a fittingly monstrous word for the study of monsters, the last creatures to be visited are those most odd refugees from reason known as the Marvels of the East. These outrageous creatures were foisted on Europe by the Greeks, to whom we owe much of our early knowledge of the East. For it was Ktesias, a well-educated Greek physician practicing at a Persian court of the fourth century B.C., who perpetrated much of this nonsense, which he claimed originated in India. As we shall see, it was certainly a lesser part of the glory that was Greece. If nothing else, it ranks high in the catalogue of tall tales told by travelers.

Moving along nicely under their own power for almost five hundred years, many of the monsters found their way into a novel of the second century of the Christian era, known as the *Romance of Alexander*. From then on they appear and reappear in the art and literature of Europe right up into the eighteenth century. We have selected for our illustrations a number of the monsters illustrated in the woodcuts of Schedel's *Chronicle of the World*, published in Nürnberg in 1498, and in later works. Among the more fabulous are the cynocephali, or dogheaded, barking men; the one-eyed arimaspians of Scythia, singularly ill equipped for their labors of filching gold from gryphons; a headless horror with its face on its chest; the sciapods, whose only leg ended in an enormous foot, which could be used as an umbrella to shade them from the sun; the martikhora, or lion with an almost human head; and the crane man (Figs. 174–178).

We have little cause to feel superior to this nonsense. The boardwalks, midways, and country fairs of today alone bear witness to our gullibility. The citizens continue to pay out their hard-earned money to see fake monsters far inferior in creative imagination to the Marvels of the East. Wittkower says in his fascinating paper on this subject:

Monsters—composite beings, half-human, half-animal—play a part in the thought and imagery of all people at all times. Everywhere the monster has been credited with the powers of a god or the diabolical forces of evil. Monsters have had their share in mythologies and fairy-tales, superstitions and prognostications. In the *Marvels of the East* this old demonic inheritance was at the same time preserved and made pseudo-rational. But their ethnological shadow existence sank back into the sphere of magic whenever the innate awe of the monster came to the fore.*

STRANGE DEITIES

The pantheons of all civilizations have their grotesque and fantastic gods, but none more strange than those of Tibet. Buddhism reached this Himalayan country in the seventh century of the Christian era. By this time its followers and practitioners had separated into two sects. One school, Hinayana, followed the simple teachings of their founder, the North Indian prince, Gautama; the other, Mahayana, absorbed local deities and gave great weight to ritual and faith. The Mahayana school triumphed in Tibet in the following century by absorbing the entire pantheon of gods and demons of the local religion, known as Pon.

The American authorities on Tibetan iconography, Gordon and Clark, whose writings are the source of much of what follows, have devoted considerable study to the bewildering and complex population of the Lamaist pantheon. There is still no exact census of the inmates; but there appear to be at least nine hundred of them. It is not for us to go into a classification of the strange-looking citizens of this pantheon. It is enough to note that most of what is thoroughly grotesque and fantastic to our eyes is indigenous or of Tántric origin (figures with more than the usual number of heads, arms, or legs). A number of these deities, such as Mahakala (Fig. 179), are of particular interest for the purpose of this writing. It could never be said of the Tibetans that they created their gods in their own image.

*Wittkower: "Marvels of the East" in the *Journal* of the Warburg and Courtauld Institute (London, 1942) Vol. 5, p. 197.

Very fearsome-looking are the Yi-dam, or tutelary deities. Especially so are the Dhyani Buddhas, who are always represented in sexual embrace with their Shakti, or female energy. Less fearsome, but equally weird, are the eighty-four Great Magicians, some of whom are known as Flying Sorcerers (Figs. 180–182).

The late great orientalist, A. K. Coomaraswamy, pointed out that the fearsome-looking deities are often not that way at all. Such a one is Yamantaka, who assumed his ferocious mien for the purpose of conquering Yama, the god of death (Figs. 183 and 184). Small figurines of Yamantaka and his Shakti are stock household furnishings in many parts of China. Fearsome, but only superficially so, is Lha-mo, the Glorious Goddess, one of the Defenders of the Faith (Fig. 185). She is generally shown as a blood-curdlingly savage woman and appears to be the Tibetan equivalent of the Indian Kali. She is also a manifestation of time and is the Patron of the Dalai and Tashi lamas. She is said to have been the wife of the King of Demons in Ceylon and to have tried unsuccessfully to convert her husband to Buddhism. To get even with him, she killed and ate their son.

All of the figures illustrated are of bronze, cast in the *cire perdu* process. When the artist finished his work, tiny rolls of paper or cloth bearing magic incantations and prayers, together with relics and seeds, were sealed into the base of the figurine or its stand; it then became sacred.

The terrifying appearance of Yama is belied by his story. This holy man was beheaded by robbers some seconds before he was about to achieve Nirvana. As they had just cut off the head of a stolen bull, Yama put the bull's head on his bleeding stump of a neck and forthwith consumed the two robbers. He then proceeded to eat his way through the population of Tibet. But for the intervention of Yamantaka he would have consumed the entire citizenry. Yamantaka, the Lord and Conqueror of Death, was also of kindly disposition. According to Grünwedel, he only acquired his extra heads, his thirty-four arms, and his sixteen legs in order to overpower Yama, who had shut himself up in a tower with thirty-four windows and sixteen doors.

THE ULTIMATE MONSTER—DEATH

Last and most terrifying of all monsters, because of his inevitable appearance at the final reckoning, is that unavoidable reality—Death. Man's horror of and unwillingness to accept his last enemy, death, has been great and nigh universal. His obstinacy in the face of this natural and logical development of life has led him into strange paths seeking all but the true reasons for the grisly phenomenon. Indeed, much of the support of Western religions comes from their promise of a solution to the problem. And man's struggle with this problem has resulted in works of art of breathtaking greatness and beauty, such as those of Brueghel and Dürer.

Among the more primitive societies there is a pathetic and desperate refusal to accept death as a cardinal condition of existence. This frequently results in death being attributed to evil spirits using the power of magic. With this approach it is understandable that death has been personified and given characteristics and recognizable forms. Many of these are illustrated in this book. The most obvious symbolic form of death is the skeleton. But it is by no means a universal symbol, although found in cultures and civilizations as remote and separated as Tibet, pre-Columbian Mexico, and western Europe during the past thousand years.

The ancient Greeks had several symbolic figures representing death, all of them considerably less grim than the skeleton. The best-known of these were the sword-bearing Thanatos, winged and black-robed; Hermes Psychopompos, who conducted souls to the underworld; and Hermes Psychostates, who weighed the souls of the departed. The skeleton did not appear in classic Greece as a symbol of death itself, but as a wry, almost comic figure like the *calaveras* of the Mexican Day of the Dead, to remind people to enjoy today, for who knows what the morrow holds.

No treatment of this symbol could more graphically emphasize the diametrically opposed attitudes towards life of the ancient Greeks on the one side and of the Tibetans and Aztecs on the other. For, as Weber points out in his fascinating but neglected study on aspects of death, "the study of human ideas of death derives most of its interest from human aspects of life. The aspects of the one are more or less dependent on and motivated by the aspects of the other." The figure of Death in the Tibetan and pre-Columbian civilizations is completely and utterly serious. In their iconography he assumes enormous, almost pathological, proportions. That this should be so in Tibet, whose entire population adores Gautama Sakyamuni—the Enlightened One—may seem odd, but it is certainly not unusual. History is studded with the chronicles of entirely Christian nations whose inhabitants have enthusiastically butchered one another in the name of the Prince of Peace. When Buddhism came to Tibet, it brought with it a considerable baggage of Tantric lore from India. Much of this is related to magic and to the eventual destruction of the world. To make headway in a highly competitive religious market, Buddhism had to absorb a whole pantheon of local gods of terror and death belonging to the native, animistic religion. Typical of the intensity and horror of this aspect of Tibetan Buddhism are the Citapati, the Lords of the Graveyard, who are always represented as two dancing skeletons waving masses of entrails in one hand and holding a set of eyeballs in the other (Fig. 186). The extremes of Buddhism can be seen in the contrast between these savage figures and the gentle emaciated sixth-century Buddha, who, in deep meditation, has virtually become a skeleton (Fig. 187).

The image of Death appears frequently in the art of the pre-Columbian civilizations of Central America, as witness our *Death's Head Jar* from the valley of Guatemala (Fig. 188). This is to be expected from the intensely grisly grimness with which those in power in these civilizations went about sacrificing scores of thousands of human victims. The rituals inspiring Aztec works of art throb with the pain and terror of the torn-out hearts of unnumbered victims; they reek of the blood which must have surged in a horrible stream down the steps of the Temples of the Sun. Truly, the people of the Aztec and some other pre-Cortés societies must certainly have believed that everything was for the worst in this worst of all possible worlds.

In the Western world the development and spread of the Christian ideology gave an altogether different significance to death and its symbolic representations such as the skeleton. The Hebrew concept of death as the gateway to a future life flourished and grew mightily in the conditions and world view of early Christianity. The Christian attitude to life was the rather gloomy and negative one that it is only a fitful thing, at best a preparation for the hereafter. Contemplation of the miserable material condition of Western man for a thousand years and more, his short expectation of life, his physical discomfort, his traumas from such cataclysms as the Black Death, all of these things make credible an acceptance of a negative attitude to life. It is no small wonder that much popular literature dealt with such gloomy subjects as *Memento Mori* and *Ars Moriendi*. The theme of this literature is nowhere better expressed than by the English divine Jeremy Taylor, who wrote in his *Rule and Exercise of Holy Dying*: "He that would die well must always look for death, everyday knocking at the gates of the grave; and then the gates of the grave shall never prevail against him to do him mischief."

Death in a skeleton form emerges as the medieval King of Terror, but king of a special kind of socialized terror. He is the Great Leveler of Guyot Marchand's Dance of Death, who comes for rich and poor, good and bad, pope and emperor, priest and fool. And he is ever present, ever ready to snatch his victims in the midst of life. Allegories of death, all of them intensely didactic, were tremendously popular throughout western Europe during the Middle Ages. Thus Antal writes in his monumental study of Florentine painting in the fourteenth century:

> The exhortation to man to prepare himself for the good death on which his fate hereafter depended was even more often combined with reflections on the vanity of all earthly existence, with ideas expressing dissatisfaction with the prevailing state of affairs, and with the conception of the great leveller, Death. The skeleton and the putrefying corpse were the chief motives of this "democratic" world of thought and its art.*

Death, the Great Leveler and the King of Terror, is the theme of some extraordinary paintings by, or attributed to, great masters like Grünewald, Nikolaus Manuel-Deutsch, Baldung-Grien, Dürer, and Brueghel (Figs. 189–195). Browning's observation about

*Antal: *Florentine Painting and its Social Background* (London: Kegan Paul, 1947).

himself that "the life in me abolished the death in things" can very appropriately be applied to these works, such is their authority and timelessness.

Although the subject of Death the Grim Reaper—very often the symbolic figures of Death and Time are merged—appears in Italian art, the compost of Italian history could not fertilize it as successfully as that of northern Europe. The emergence of this essentially medieval attitude towards death into the more rational atmosphere of Renaissance Europe sheds significant light on man's intellectual development. Illuminating examples of this more rational if somewhat dramatized attitude towards death are Marcadente da Ravenna's *Allegory of Death* (Fig. 196), John of Calcar's engraving of the so-called *Thinking Skeleton* for Vesalius' famous work on anatomy (Fig. 197), and the pair of delicate and charming *Skeleton Ornaments* by Monogramist B. H. M. (Figs. 198 and 199).

With Holbein's version of the Dance of Death—perhaps the best-known—we are still largely dealing with the medieval King of Terror, the Great Reaper who swings his indiscriminate scythe, reminding the world that in the midst of life we are in death (Figs. 200 and 201). But with the outstanding giants of the Northern Renaissance, such as Dürer and Brueghel, there is a marked change in the interpretation of the theme of death. It now has much more philosophical content, reflecting the widening of man's intellectual horizon and his deeper penetration into the nature of the world, made possible by the Renaissance and the development of humanism.

Two of Dürer's most famous works treat of death. One is the drawing *King Death on a Horse* in the British Museum, generally regarded as one of the greatest charcoal drawings ever made (Fig. 202). The other is that master engraving called *Knight, Death, and Devil*, which Panofsky, the great Dürer scholar, shows to have been inspired by a work of Erasmus (Figs. 7 and 192). Here for the first time in a major work the subjects of death and the Devil are not treated as overwhelming and real. What Dürer is saying is that the sleep of faith produces monsters. This constituted advanced thinking for that day and age and leads logically to the rationalism of Goya. The passage of the great Rotterdam humanist Erasmus, which Dürer brilliantly translates into graphic terms, deals with the problems besetting the rational Christian as he goes through this world.

In order that you [Christian Knight] may not be deterred from the path of virtue because it seems rough and dreary, because you may have to renounce the comforts of the world and because you must constantly fight three unfair enemies, the flesh, the devil, and this world, this . . . rule shall be proposed to you: All those spooks and phantoms which come upon you as in the very gorges of Hades must be deemed for nought.

The other great philosophical painting of the Northern Renaissance which deals with the macabre theme is Brueghel the Elder's *Triumph of Death* (Figs. 193–195).

There are few works in the whole history of western European painting so full of content as this great treasure of the Prado. Just as Michelangelo's *Last Judgment* is definitive and made it impossible and unnecessary for any further attempt to deal with that subject, so Peter Brueghel's *Triumph of Death* says all that can possibly be said on that subject. If the *Triumph of Death* were the only surviving work by Brueghel, we would know immediately that it was painted by a master as great in his field as Balzac in the field of the novel. Unfortunately, the appellation of "Peasant" has done much to obscure a correct appreciation of the stature and quality of this northern Titan. For he is anything but an ingenuous painter of the simple. He is a painter-genius of complex and cultivated mind, a humanist who used the tools of naturalistic symbolism to add tremendous depth to reality.

A study of the works of Brueghel brings home the truth of that unhappy but obstinate fact that the more you know the more you become aware of how much more there is to know. This quality of Brueghel is revealed in all of his works. His picture of the world is so real and so enormous that we are immediately made conscious that there is much more we do not understand or are incapable at that moment of understanding. This quality is something quite apart from the difficulty of comprehending some of his symbolic language, which was clear to his contemporaries. He makes his observations on the real world in an extremely modern way. For, as Hauser points out, "Brueghel's world-view is . . . self-conscious and unspontaneous . . . not merely in the sense of the reflectiveness common to all post-Renaissance art, but also in the sense that the artist presents not a description of reality in general, but consciously and intentionally presents *his* version, *his* interpretation of reality, and in the sense that all his work could be summed up under the heading 'How I see it.' This is the revolutionary novelty and the eminently modern feature . . . in the art of Brueghel."

A true and full appreciation of this Flemish master began only a few years ago. Until the beginning of this century there were no works of Brueghel on display in any gallery in the English-speaking world. A great debt is owed to scholars like Dvořák and Tolnay for their labors in making possible a revaluation of the first and greatest of the Brueghels.

Much of the post-Brueghel treatment of the theme of death in Western civilization has been anticlimax. We have already pointed out that nothing significant remained to be said on the subject. Lesser artists, like the unknown sixteenth-century German woodcarver, Valdés Leal, Ligozzi, Della Bella, Gamelin, and the unknown Spanish woodcarver, have restated the old truths in their individual ways (Figs. 203–208). A few masters, like Rowlandson and Daumier, used the conventional skeleton image of death in the arsenal of satirical weapons which they launched against the stupidities, indecencies, and injustices of their times (Figs. 209 and 210). So, in a smaller and less artistic way, did Posada (Fig. 211). The romantics and later the decadents frequently used the skeleton of death to raise goosepimples on the overfed torsos of the much-despised bourgeoisie. With Wiertz and Munch, this is sensational, if not melodramatic (Figs. 212 and 213), with Ensor, quaintly whimsical (Fig. 214). With others, like Bresdin, it is the symbol of their tiredness of the ugly bourgeois world (Fig. 215). It is not that people no longer believe in death. In the Western world, at least, except on feast days, people are far too busy with the material problems of living to ponder long on the condition and fate of their souls. Or, like Balzac, they have come to see that "death is certain; let us forget it."

Nightmares, Dreams And Other Fantasies

WE WILL NOW MAKE A SHORT EXCURSION INTO THAT VAST WORLD of art works conceived by wild and unrestrained fantasy, in which also nightmares and dreams are engendered. But first we will find it useful to explore a little the nature of dreams. Many writers have tried their hands at showing the relationship between art and dreams. Some of the more reasonable guesses came out of the fertile mind of the late Wolfgang Born. We have made free use of his interesting writings in the section which follows.

The phenomenon of the dream and the problem of its interpretation have been of considerable interest to mankind since the beginning of recorded history. The unknown authors of the first written records—the citizens of the Egyptian and Tigris-Euphrates civilizations—were greatly exercised by this subject. Already at that early date man reasoned that dreams do not come out of thin air; they must have some cause. He hit on the idea that dreams come from God. Logically, then, the priests were best equipped to interpret them. For even in those days dreams came in shapes as strange as those of today. From our point of vantage over the pre-logical thinkers we can see that the ancients overemphasized the prophetic value of dreams. But even there they had found something, as the psychologists who later studied intuition were to learn.

Writers in the classical world of Greece and Rome, much of whose knowledge and ideas about dreams came from the Middle East, dealt with the dream as part of the universe in which both the gods and man adventured. Homer, Virgil, Ovid, Lucian, and Cicero each produced writings in which during a dream the soul went on long journeys into the nether world or into outer space. These writings inspired very little in the plastic arts, and what they did inspire is not very interesting; but they incubated for a long time and during the Renaissance hatched out, directly inspiring many pictorial works.

At the same time Greek philosophers such as those of the Pythagorean School, and Heraclitus, Democritus, Plato, and Aristotle, all contributed interesting and sometimes penetratingly accurate theories about the dream. Plato made an amazingly correct observation concerning sleep. In *The Republic* he pointed out that "in all of us, even in good men, there is a lawless wild-beast nature, which peers out in sleep." He claimed also that, if passion or desire dominated reason during sleep, the dreams which took place would be unpleasant; if reason dominated, the dreams would be sensible. Aristotle, too, wrote much on dreams and explained clearly what is known today as the prodromal dream, or dream caused by physical stimuli such as noise, heat, cold, and stomach-ache. The Greek physicians Hippocrates and Galen followed this thought and used dreams as an aid to diagnosis.

In the early part of the Christian era a Greek named Artemidorus wrote a book on dream interpretation which became famous. Although it followed most of the then known theories of dreams, it achieved its popularity through its handy list of dream subjects and their meaning, particularly their foretelling of the future. Dream books influenced by Artemidorus were commonly used throughout the Middle Ages. With Albertus Magnus and his contemporaries, dream interpretation was given complicated depth by the addition of many elements of alchemy and astrology.

The beginning of the modern, scientific approach to dreams can be seen in the writings of Renaissance investigators like Cardano and Paracelsus. Indeed, Theophrastus Bombastus von Hohenheim, to give the remarkable Paracelsus his full name, anticipated the Freudians with his theory of the nightmare. He said that little demons called *incubi* and *succubae* caused these unpleasant dreams. *Incubi* were demon lovers who visited sleeping women, sometimes destroying them, such was the ardor of their passion. A dictionary specializing in such matters points out that they were handsome and virile but were subject to "such drawbacks as cloven feet and an evil smell." The fastidious and the less venturesome could keep them off with St. John's-wort and dill. The female of the species, the *succuba*, was less deadly than the male.

Though held within the colorful but narrow frontiers of sixteenth-century thought, Paracelsus still had great insight. He saw what the Freudians were able to see hundreds of years later, that *incubi* and *succubae* were nothing more than sexual fantasies which the imagination hatched out during sleep. The oppressive feeling of the nightmare was caused by the conflict between desire and inhibition.

The groundwork was laid for the scientific study of dreams in the nineteenth century. First there was the philosophical stimulus of the romantics Novalis and Nerval; later came the medical explorers such as Carus. Then came the psychoanalysts, of whom Freud has made the most significant single contribution.

Freud tells us that all the erotic and other impulses which we are trained to repress from our everyday life seep out during our dreams in disguised shapes. The "superego," which is nothing more than our training and social conditioning, forces them into these disguises or symbolic shapes. What takes place in our dreams is imaginary wish-fulfillment, the wishes frequently being erotic.

The unacceptable or repressed wishes disguise themselves in three ways. They may appear in the imagery of the dream not as themselves but as distantly connected. This is known as displacement. Or many of the images directly reflecting the suppressed wishes may be combined into a single image. This is known as condensation. Or many of the images relating to the repressed wishes may appear as symbols. Freud believed that a further process takes place. He said that the dream as dreamed is screened through the fore-conscious. Only a "dramatized" part of it is remembered on waking. He called this the "manifest" content of the dream and distinguished it from the "latent" content, the part that the psychoanalysts were after.

Other workers in the field have added to or broadened Freud's theory to take into account their own observations and experience. Adler and Jung were more concerned, each in his own way, with the struggle to exist rather than with erotic phenomena. Jung gives far more importance to the role of the irrational in man's waking and sleeping life than Adler and regards dreams as an "expression of the wisdom of the unconscious."

Fromm and the late Harry Stack Sullivan, explorers of the human psyche who were blessed with sweet reasonableness and an awareness that man does not live in a social vacuum, believe that dreams are both rational and irrational. In waking life, they tell us, man is mainly concerned with mastering his environment or defending himself in it or against it. When he is asleep, he is free of this struggle and can be concerned entirely with himself and his inner world. His dreams—that is, his mind working during sleep, aptly called the "brother of death"—are subject to a special logic which is different from that of the waking state. It is a logic "in which not time and space are the ruling categories but intensity and association." Fromm goes on to show the similarity between dreams and "the oldest creations of man—myth," both of which are written in the same language of symbols.

Another worker in this field, Joseph Campbell, calls the dream a personalized myth and the myth a depersonalized dream. He attributes tremendous importance to the role of the myth in man's history. "It would not be too much to say," he writes, "that myth is the secret opening through which the inexhaustible energies of the cosmos pour into human cultural manifestation. Religions, philosophies, arts, the social forms of primitive and historic man, prime discoveries in science and technology, the very dreams that blister sleep, boil up from the basic, magic ring of myth."

This world of myth is peopled by Geza Roheim's "Eternal Ones of the Dream." Some of these "Eternal Ones" can be seen in our illustrations: in the predynastic Egyptian figures (Fig. 216); in the Harappa and Zhob valley figurines (Figs. 217 and 218); in the Mesopotamian figure and cylinder seal (Figs. 219 and 220); in the pre-Columbian pottery jars from Peru and Costa Rica (Figs. 221–223); in the Navajo sand painting for the *Male Shooting Arrow Chant* (Fig. 224); and in the bark paintings and wooden figures of the Australian aborigines among whom Roheim did much of his work (Figs. 225–227).

The appeal of grotesque and fantastic art to modern man is based in some measure on its resemblance, whether or not superficial, to the world of sleep, dreams, and myths. Fromm and other psychologists have shown that there is sense in the world of nightmares, dreams, and fantasies. No longer can we say with older generations that dreams are pure poppycock. And so it is with grotesque and fantastic art, a subject which has come to interest us seriously only within recent years. It is the solid ground put under dreams by Freud, Fromm, and a host of others in between which has made this possible. Fromm's contribution has, by its admixture of brilliant insight with restrained common sense, torn down most of the arcane veil through which the dream world appeared mysterious, incomprehensible, if not completely chaotic.

The enlightened today have perhaps gone to the opposite extreme, and their overstressing of significance in dreams can often raise obstacles to an understanding and appreciation of grotesque and fantastic elements in art.

If, to paraphrase Freud, the interpretation of dreams is the royal road to the understanding of grotesque and fantastic art, it puts us only at the first milestone. For the road is long and tortuous. To make any distance on this road, the traveler must also come equipped with a broad knowledge of anthropology, folklore, culture history, art history, and economic, political, and religious history. Unfortunately, brilliant minds like those of Dvořák, Focillon, Tolnay, Benesch, and the scholars of the Warburg

Institute come only at rare intervals. And when we consider that sizable volumes have been published to interpret single fantastic paintings of Bosch and Brueghel alone—*The Garden of Earthly Delights*, or *Millennium*, and *Flemish Proverbs*—we can readily understand that it will be some time before we are helped far along this road. Our concern here is to aid the would-be traveler by placing the guideposts of reason and common sense at the start of his journey.

Now, while all of the theories and observations concerning dreams and myths shed some light on fantasy in art, a strict Freudian interpretation only loses us in a psycho-analytical bog of insignificant trivia. We run the same risk that the Italian scholar Mario Praz ran when he wrote his fascinating study of the decadent movement, *The Romantic Agony*. He pointed out that the writer who deals with such subject matter as decadence (or grotesque and fantastic art) is likely to be classed with those who are concerned only with the mentally sick. This error, alas, is only too easy to make. And it creates in every direction an unfavorable atmosphere for piecing together "the universal human background which is visible behind the paroxysms" of the distraught.

The subject, then, is too important to leave to the psychoanalysts. For to interpret the works of such artists as Bosch, Brueghel, and Goya in terms of "infantile, irrational desires" sheds more light on psychoanalysts and their world than it does on the life and world of these artists. Thus it is possible that the symbols which appear time and time again in the grotesque and fantastic art of the late Middle Ages and early Renaissance had the same meaning then as now. For example, the knives and tortures were outward and visible trappings of inward and spiritual anxieties. That is hardly new. After all, quavering in the human soul has been going on for thousands of years, back down the corridors of time to the point where man could hardly be differentiated from the other higher mammals. But in the western Europe of the fifteenth and sixteenth centuries there was less abracadabra than today. Everyone who saw the fantasies of ·Bosch, Brueghel, and their followers knew that the knives were for the punishment of the sinners. The man of today who dreams himself into a Sheffield-Solingen nightmare takes his mystification to a highly paid technician for an interpretation which, in the Middle Ages, he who ran might read.

Sometimes, as in life, we have our nightmares while we are awake. Da Vinci's *Grotesque Heads*, unfortunates sketched from life, are examples of the walking night-mare which hardly calls for interpretation (Figs. 228 and 229).

We must never forget that the mystery, irrationality, and inexplicability of much of the grotesque and fantastic exist for us alone, and not for their creators and their original, initiated audience. Indeed, our lack of understanding brings to mind the observation of Novalis: "I heard it said that unintelligibility results only from a failure of the intelligence; a limited intelligence looks only for what it has already and so never gets any farther." What appears as myth and mystery to us was everyday life to the man of the Middle Ages, who knew far more of the geography of the other world than his descendant does of the topography of the county he lives in. But, then, we are apt to give more social recognition today to an "amateur" tennis star than to the translator of a Sanskrit classic, more to the memory of Buffalo Bill Cody than to Francis of Assisi.

That artists have been interested in exploring dreams and nightmares is little cause for wonder. For in artists the powers of visual imagination and fantasy are more highly developed than in any other people, excepting possibly poets. The interest is more often covert than overt. But there are clear exceptions. These we can see in the so-called *Dream of Raphael* of Marcantonio Raimondi (Fig. 230) and in the so-called *Melancholy of Michelangelo* of Gisi (Fig. 231). Let it not be thought that these two works are just wild dreams. They are full of esoteric meaning and are shot through with references to Neoplatonic and alchemical thought, Greek natural philosophy, and elements of Greek and Near Eastern mysticism. Less complicated are the *Odd Dreams of Panta-gruel*, attributed to Rabelais (Figs. 232–236); Guido Maria Mitelli's *Dream Alphabet* (Figs. 237 and 238); Goya's key work, *The Sleep of Reason Produces Monsters* (Fig. 239); Fuseli's *Nightmare* (Fig. 240); and Grandville's and Kubin's eerie or terrifying works (Figs. 241–244).

By their very titles these artists tell us that they are dealing with the world of dreams. Goya's own handwritten notes on recently discovered sketches made as preparation for both the *Caprichos* and the *Proverbios* now show that he was illustrating his dreams. The sketch for the famous *Sleep of Reason* plate has this notation on it: "The artist dreaming. His only purpose is to banish harmful, vulgar beliefs, and to perpetuate, in this work of caprices, the solid testimony of truth." Referring to this, López-Rey, in his brilliant and definitive study on the *Caprichos*, says that "one cannot help seeing in that a rationalist attitude, whatever those who have looked at the *Caprichos* from a romantic, realist, or surrealist point of view may claim." Here, then, our subject matter is dreams, but dreams with a didactic purpose. The mystery of such plates as *The Double-faced Woman, The Giant,* and *Flying Men* fades if we keep this ever in mind (Figs. 245–247). To explain their fantastic character, let us quote the highly literate Goya once more.

The imitation of nature is as difficult as it is admirable when one succeeds in doing so. But some credit must be given to the artist who, holding aloof from her, has represented forms or movements that to this day have existed only in the imagination. . . . Painting, like poetry, selects from the world whatever it considers suitable for its purposes. It unites, in a single fantastic being, qualities and characteristics that nature has divided among many. Thanks to this creative combination, the artist is no longer a servile copyist but an inventor.

Bosch and Brueghel are two other great masters whose work is closely connected with the world of dreams. They, too, have a strong didactic bent. Bosch, the master of the nightmare, is concerned in most of his works with flaying knaves and charlatans and with scaring the wits out of wantons. His pictures of the torments of Hell get many of their most startling ideas from the long poem called *The Dream of Tondale*. The torments which man suffers when he is at war with himself are shown most graphically in details from the *Temptation of St. Anthony*, the *Hay Wagon*, and the *Garden of Earthly Delights*, or *Millennium* (Figs. 248–254). Similarly, there is a dream quality about much of Brueghel's work. Bosch and Brueghel were equally concerned about man's fate while here on earth, and particularly with the subject of Folly, which was very popular in their day. Anticipating Goya, whom they undoubtedly influenced, they believed, as he did, that social criticism is a responsibility of the artist. In this sense there is a striking bond between them. For they selected (and we will let Goya speak once more) "from the large number of follies and blunders common in all societies, and from the vulgar prejudices and lies authorized by custom, ignorance or interest, those subjects thought most suitable for ridicule as well as for exercising the . . . fancy."

There are scores of works less overtly connected with the dream world but displaying some or all of the Freudian characteristics of the dream—displacement, condensation, symbolism, and dramatization. Some of these works, like those of Bosch and Brueghel, we have mentioned already. But in addition, and this is very important, these artists were concerned with problems of society. Social criticism and commentary appear in the *Ship of Fools*, the *Tree Man*, the *Battle of the Money Bags*, *Everyman*, and the *Battle Between Fasting and Feasting* (Figs. 255–259). In his daring *Hay Wagon*, Bosch openly attacks the masters of his world. He shows pope and emperor, clergy and princes, following the train of the great wagon—symbol of sin—and hard bound for Hell (Fig. 253). Also concerned with the disorders and problems of society is the remarkable illuminated manuscript known as the *Tree of Battles*, in the Royal Library of Brussels (Fig. 260). Direct social comment is made in such works as Piero di Cosimo's illustration of a poem of Ovid, *The Discovery of Honey* (Fig. 261). This charming work is a satiric observation on the early condition of man. Equally concerned with the peculiarities of society are Mantegna's *Triumph of Virtue over Vice* (Fig. 262); Master E. S.'s *Letter M* from his *Fantastic Alphabet* (Fig. 263); Baldung-Grien's *Phyllis and Aristotle*, with its comment on the nagging wife (Fig. 264); the follower of Bosch concerned with the problem of *Feast and Fast* (Fig. 265); Van Meckenem's *Hares Roasting a Hunter* (Fig. 266); Veneziano's *Carcass*, said to represent the scourge of malaria (Fig. 267); Adriaen Pietersz Van de Venne's *Fishers of Souls* (Fig. 268), with its extraordinary and almost aloof comment on the religious struggle of the seventeenth-century Netherlands; Myle's *Noah's Ark* (Fig. 269); Audran's rococo fantasy *Singeries de Marly* (Fig. 270); Hogarth's *Bathos*, and *Credulity, Superstition, and Fanaticism*, and *Principal Inhabitants of the Moon* (Figs. 271–273); Morghen's *Moon Scenes* (Fig. 274); Blake's typical *Promise of the Redemption* (Fig. 275); Cruikshank's *Worship of Bacchus* (Fig. 276); and Kley's *Pfui, Devil!* and *England Wins* (Figs. 277 and 278).

Other artists are more concerned with private terrors and anxieties. In their works we can see the operation of one or more parts of the Freudian dream mechanism: Giovanni di Paolo's *Miracle of St. Nicholas* (Fig. 279); Gheyn's *Fantastic Heads* (Fig. 280); Magnasco's *Hermit in a Landscape* (Fig. 281); Piranesi's *Imaginary Prison* (Fig. 282); Méryon's *Ministry of Marine* (Fig. 283); Moreau's *Orpheus* (Fig. 284); Redon's *Heavenly Eye* (Fig. 285); Munch's *The Cry* (Fig. 286); and Dali's *Rhinoceros* (Fig. 287). Other works which illustrate the mechanism of dreams have been dealt with elsewhere in this book. This has been done because they more appropriately illuminate some subject in which grotesque and fantastic elements are weighty or quite significant —Hell, the Last Judgment, the temptation of St. Anthony, or monsters.

But there are further works also connected with the world of dreams, if in less obvious ways. Perhaps their meaning escapes us because it is too obvious. We must not forget that latterly we have been trained to find the esoteric, the hidden, and the subtle, rather than to recognize the obvious. In this category is much of pure grotesque decoration. It has a long and varied history, having been discovered or rediscovered during the Renaissance. Excavations in Rome at the beginning of the sixteenth century unearthed the so-called *Casa Aurea* of Nero. The walls of this and of other excavated rooms—called *grotti* by the Italians—were covered with fresco paintings of strange but very decorative combinations of animals, birds, fruit, flowers, plants, and mythological figures. Raphael, Giulio Romano, and other artists were fascinated by these decorative discoveries and immediately introduced them into their works. From that point on, this style of decoration spread throughout most of the arts.

Related, too, to the world of dreams are such works as the late thirteenth-century *Vierge Ouvrante* (Fig. 288); the fantastic Romanesque column from Souillac (Fig. 289); Flötner's *Human Alphabet* (Fig. 290); Jamnitzer's *Grotesque Ornament* (Fig. 291); Wendel Dieterlin the Younger's *Fantastic Ornament* (Fig. 292); Arcimboldo's *Fire* and *Water* (Figs. 293 and 294); Callot's *Dwarfs Sawing a Glass of Wine* (Fig. 295); Braccelli's etching from his *Bizaries* (Fig. 296); Bouda's *Fantastic Alphabet* (Fig. 297); and the anonymously modeled terra cotta statuette from the Lake Chad culture, which illustrates a whole tendency in the art of primitive peoples (Fig. 298). Not for nothing did that extraordinary eighteenth-century romantic, Fuseli, point out that "one of the most unexplored regions of art are dreams."

Envoy

WE HAVE NOW COME TO THE END OF OUR TRIP THROUGH SOME OF the wild country of sleeping reason. We have completed our tour of the Devil's realm, whose landscape blazes into life as the intellect sinks into sleep. This has been largely an economy tour, for a full exploration of the flora, fauna, and general topography of his realm would require much time and the aid of a giant Baedeker. But we have seen the principal sights: the better-known faces of the Lord of Unreason; his numerous staff; his domains; and his works. We have even included in our rapid tour a short excursion down the stream of man's subconscious by glass-bottomed boat, from which we have caught a glimpse of some of his nightmares, dreams, and fantasies.

It is not by chance that at this point in the 1960's when man's potential for destruction almost escapes comprehension, we should be making this strange and unsentimental journey. We have already remarked that the wild and fantastic world which germinates when reason sleeps has always fascinated and attracted ordinary mortals. The great French scholar Marcel Brion points out that real monsters do not fit comfortably into the neat world of reason. Sometimes reason likes to hide them or pretends to ignore them. In the last thirty years the super-monsters of unreason—Fascism, Nazism, and Stalinism—have been only too real, and could neither be hidden nor ignored. As they recede into history, their place has been taken by the ever-present threat of nuclear holocaust. This last mega-monster is too immense and paralyzingly awesome for the intellectual grasp of ordinary mortals. Like the air, it is with us whether we open or close our eyes. The simplest thing we can do is try to ignore it—and get on with the business of living.

Since Hiroshima we have seen a growing interest in grotesque and fantastic art. Our bibliography shows that exhibitions of this art and publications devoted to one or another aspect of it are now common. This present interest has one singular advantage over that other and ultimate product of sleeping reason, the Bomb. At worst Devils, Monsters, and Nightmares can make you mentally ill; but they cannot atomize you.

Plates

Delacroix inv.					Mourlot, lith. Paris

1

2

3

4

5

6

7

8

9

10

11

12

14

15

16

17

18

19

20

21

22

23

25

28

29

31

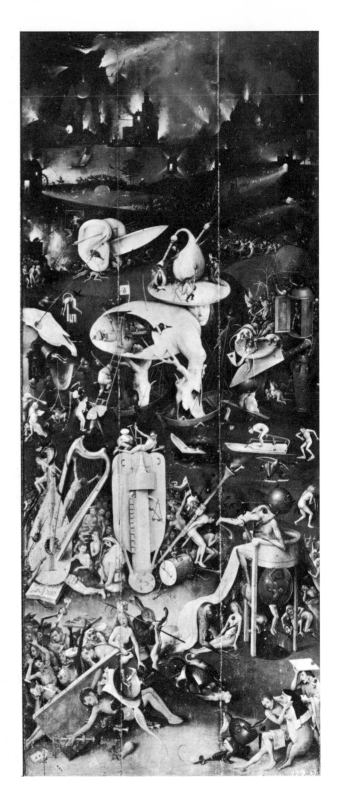

32

35

36

37

38

40

41

43

44

46

47

61

62

LVXVRIA.

Brueghel. Inuentor.
H. Cock excudebat cum priu.

LVXVRIA ENERVAT VIRES, EFFOEMINAT ARTVS

Luxurye stinckt / sÿ is vol onsuuerheden. Sÿ breeckt die Craesten / en sÿ swackt die leden

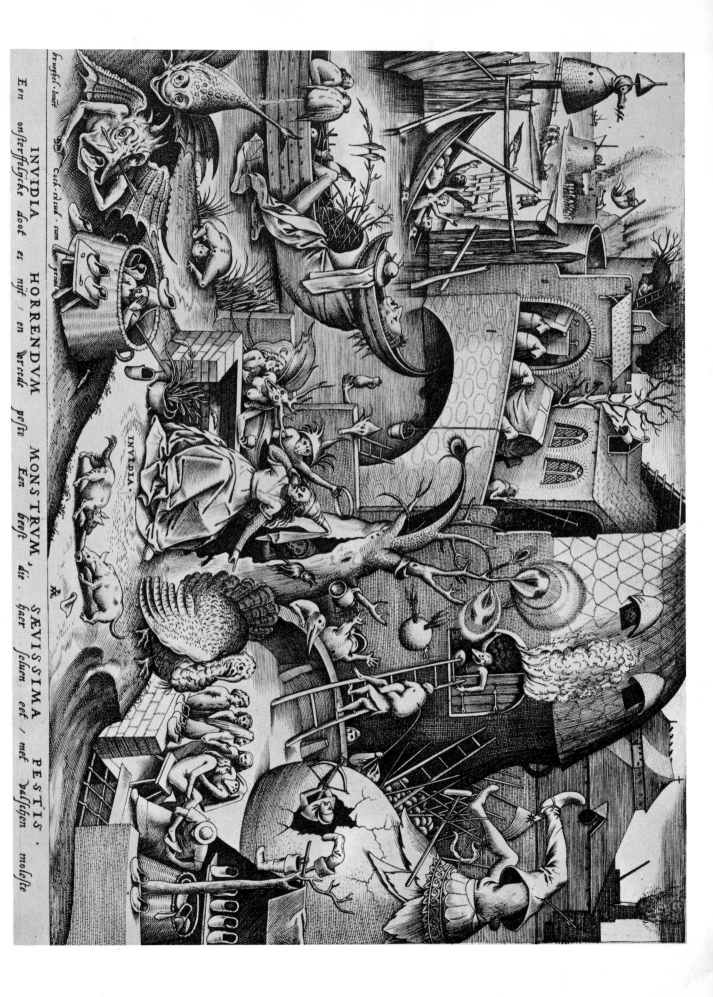

INVIDIA HORRENDVM MONSTRVM, SAEVISSIMA PESTIS.

Een onstervelijcke doot es nijt / en wreede peste Een beest die haer selven eet / met valschen molefte

bruegel. inuet. Cock. excud. cum gratia.

INVIDIA

Superbia.

Auaritia.

Luxuria.

Inuidia.

Ira.

Gula.

Pigritia.

68

69

70

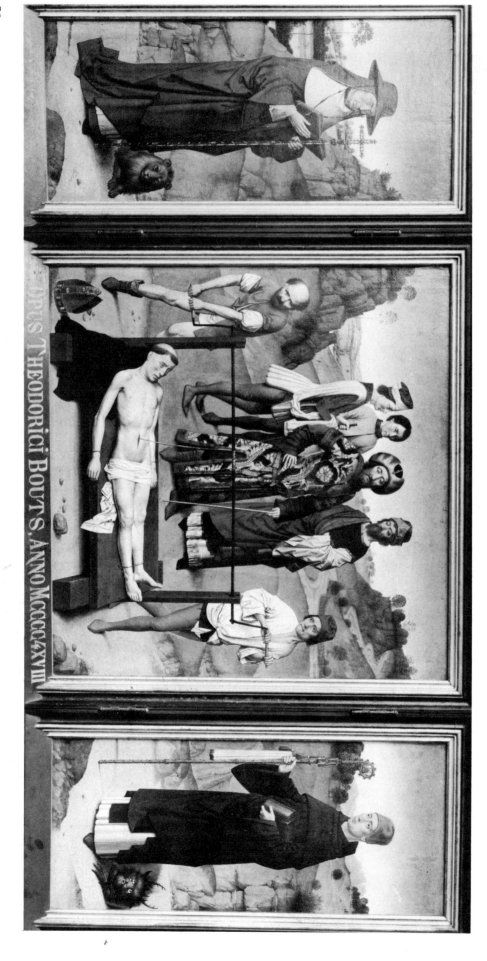

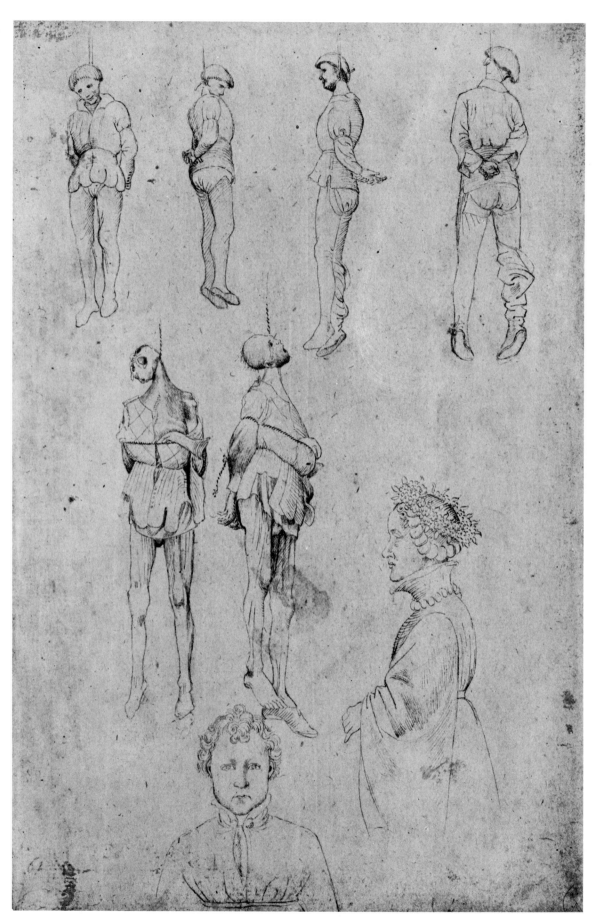

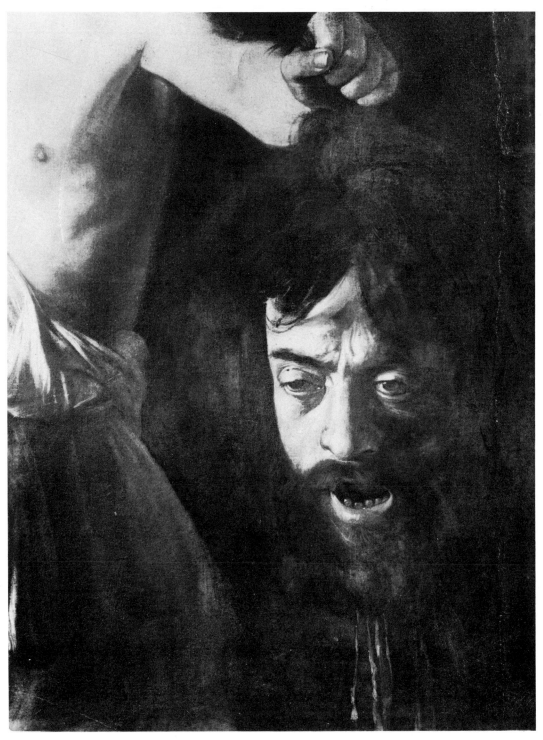

77

Ifrael ex. Cum Priuil. Reg.

L'œil touſiours ſurueillant de la duine Aſtrée   Lors que tenant l'Eſpée, et la Balance en main   Qui guette les paſſans, les meurtrit, et ſ'en iöüe,
Bannit entierement le dueil d'vne contrée.   Elle iuge et punit le voleur inhumain.   Puis luy meſme deuient le iöüet d'vne roüe.

14

78

Iſrael excud. cum Priuil. Reg.

Ce n'eſt pas ſans raiſon que les grands Cappitaines   Contre les faineants, et les Blaſphemateurs   De qui les actions par le vice aueuglées
Comme bien aduiſez. ont inuenté ces peines   Trauſtres a leur deuoir, querelleux, et menteurs   Rendent celles d'autruy laches et deſreglées.

10

79

80

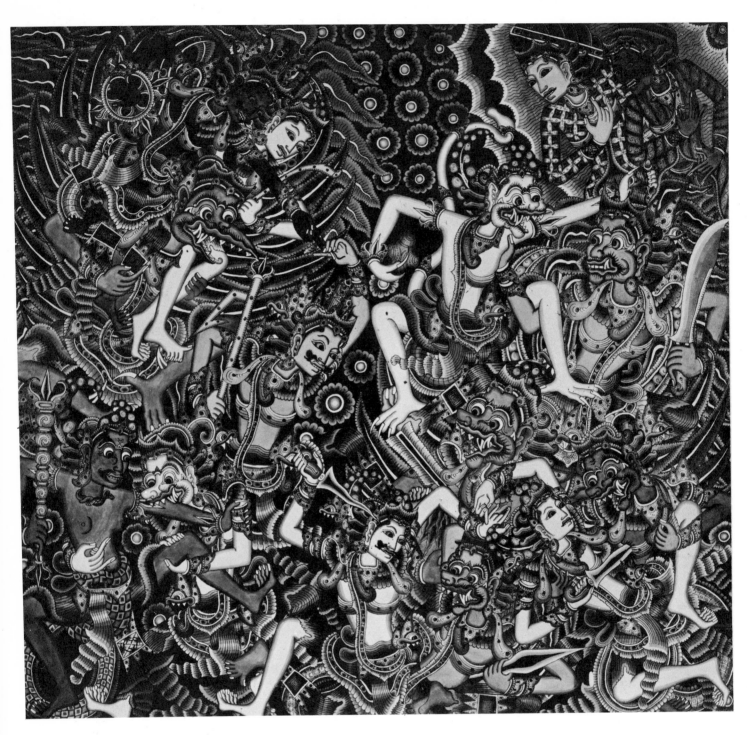

83

A la fin ces Voleurs infames et perdus , Monstrent bien que le crime (horrible et noire engeance) Et que c'est le Destin des hommes vicieux
Comme fruits malheureux a cet arbre pendus Est luy mesme instrument de honte et de vengeance , D'esprouuer tost ou tard la iustice des Cieux. 13

Israel ex. Cum Priuil. Reg.

84

Israel ex. Cum Priuil. Reg.

Voyla les beaux exploits de ces cœurs inhumains L'vn pour auoir de l'or, inuente des supplices, Et tous d'vn mesme accord commettent mechamment
Ils rauagent par tout rien nechappe a leur mains L'autre à mil forfaicts anime ses complices ; Le vol, le rapt, le meurtre, et le violement. 5

85

Israel ex. Cum Priuil. Reg.

Apres plusieurs degast par les soldats commis Les guettent à l'escart et par vne surprise Et se vengent ainsi contre ces Malheureux
A la fin les Paisans, qu'ils ont pour ennemis Les ayant mis à mort les mettent en chemise, Des pertes de leurs biens, qui ne viennent que deux. 17

86

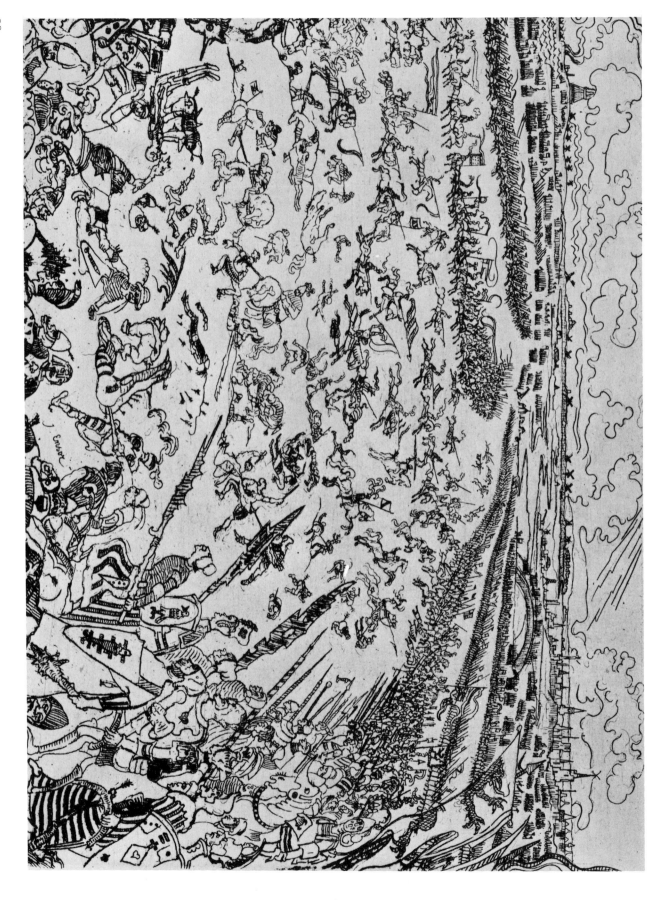

94

95

VENITE. BENEDICTI. PATRIS. MEI. IN. REGNVM. ÆTERNVM.
ITE. MALEDICTI. PATRIS. MEI. IN. IGNEM. SEMPITERNVM.

Brueghel. inuet

H. Cock. excude. cum priuileg. 1558

Compt ghy ghebenedijde mijns vaders hier.
En ghaet ghy vermaledijde in dat eewighe vier.

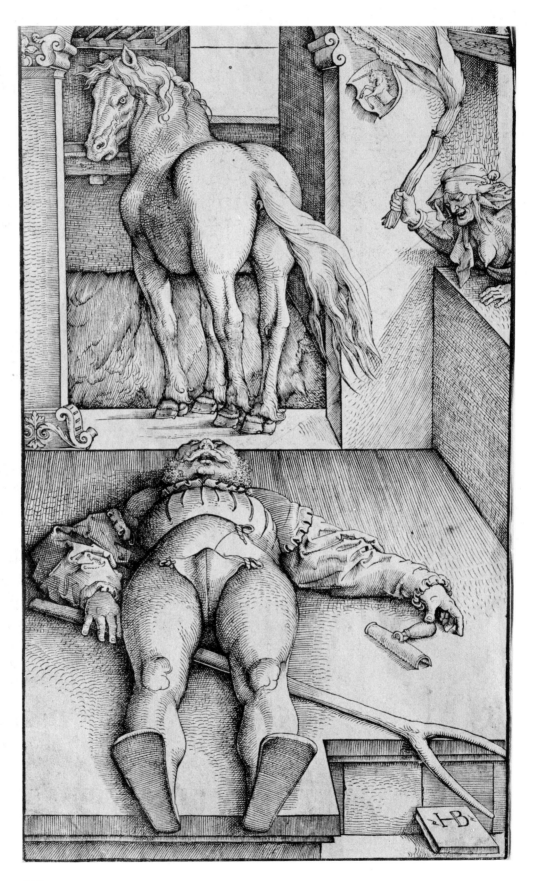

107

109

110

Linda maestra!

Donde vá mamá?

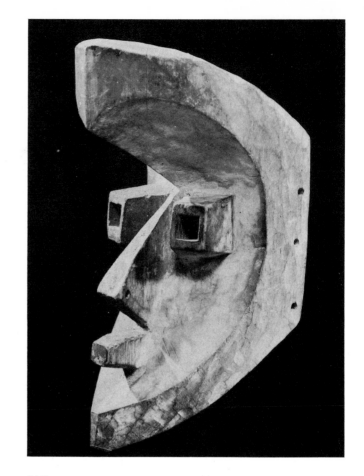

113

112

114

115

117

116

118

119

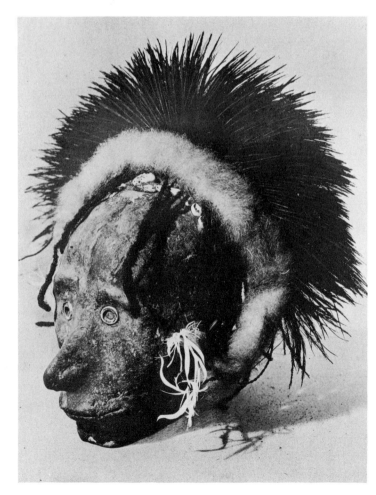

120

121

122

124

123

124

125

126

127

129

130

131

132

134

135

138

139

141

142

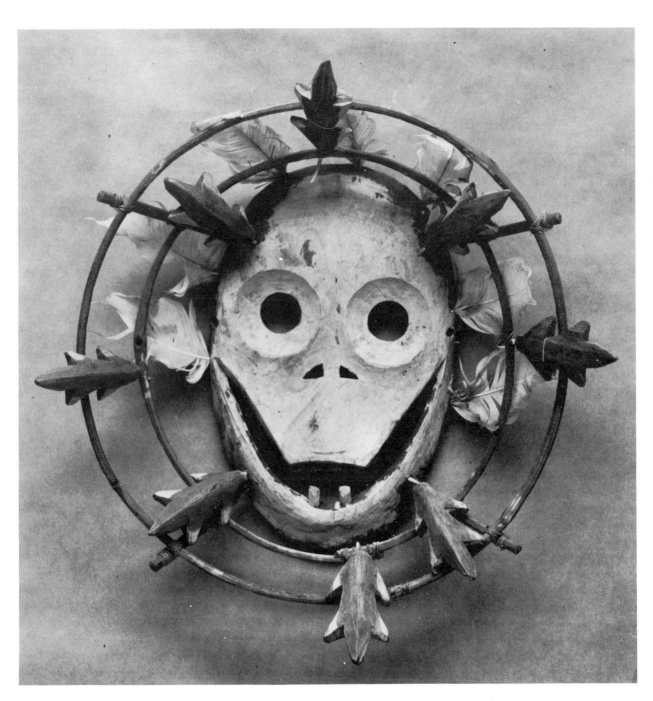

143

Cap.^o Mala Gamba.   Cap.^o Bellauita.

144

Cicho Sgarra.   Collo Francisco.

145

146

149

150

152

153

154

155

156

Dirus Agenorida laniat socia agmina Serpens, Ultor adest Cadmus pœnasq́ repoſcit ab hoste.

159

160

161

162

163

164

165

167

170

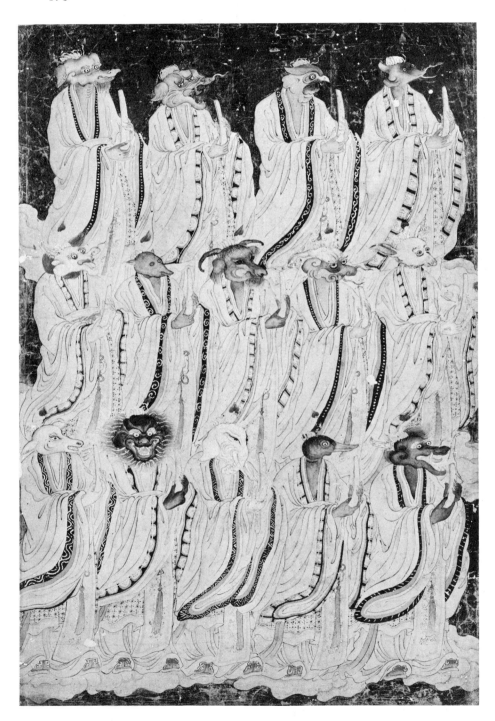

171

174

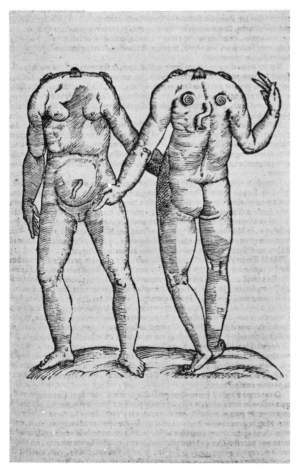

175

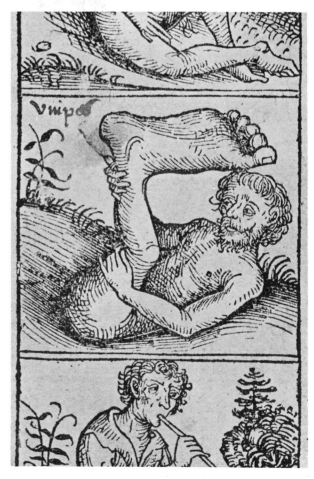

176

177

178

179

180

181

182

183

184

185

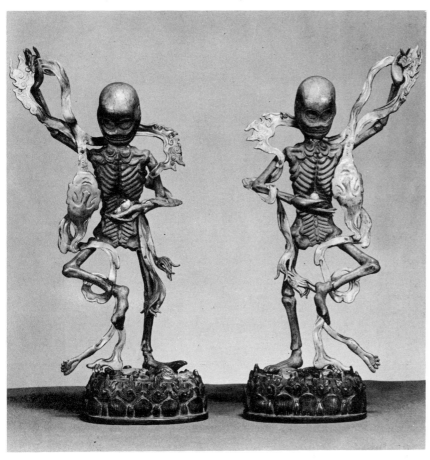

186

187

188

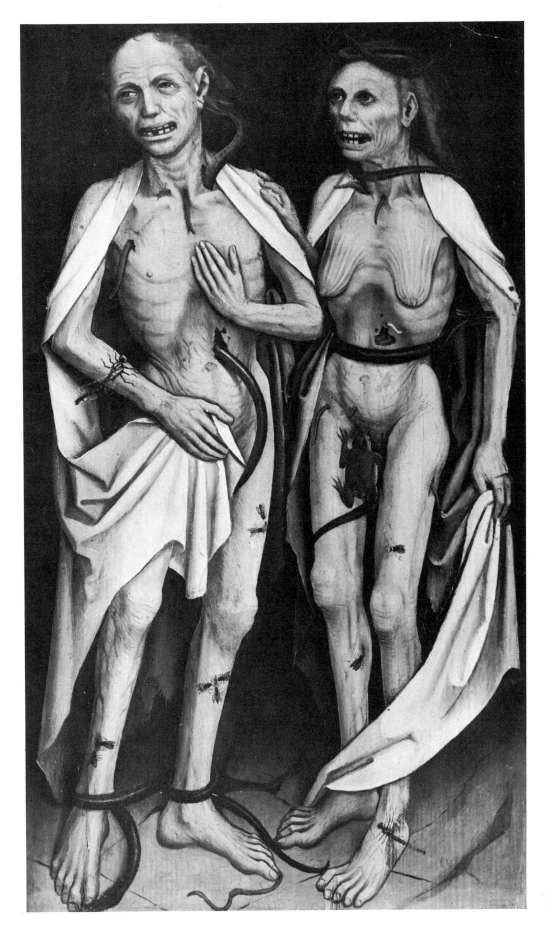

190

191

192

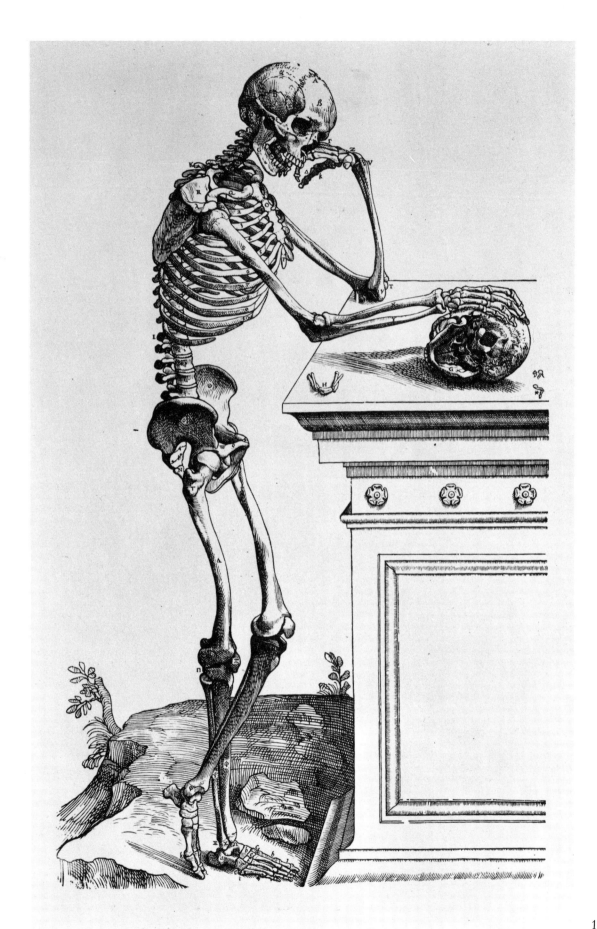

198

199

Die Keyserinn.

200

201

MEMENTO MEI 1505

202

204

Icy la Mort triomphe entre les funerailles;
Ses plus beaux promenoirs sont les lieux des batailles;
Son Throsne s'affermit de la cheute des morts;
Elle change a l'instant par ses armes subtiles,
En riuiere de sang les Campagnes fertiles,
Et les plaines de Mars en montagnes de corps.

Parmi les Escadrons, elle fait des rauages
Du tranchant de sa faux, sçauans mille passages
Caualiers et Cheuaux tombent esgalement,
& ses coups sont si prompts, q'vn puissant corps d'armée
D'vn million de corps horriblement formée
Semble n'auoir laissé q'vne ame seulement.

Ste. Villa Bella ja. et fe. cum Pri. Reg.

210

211

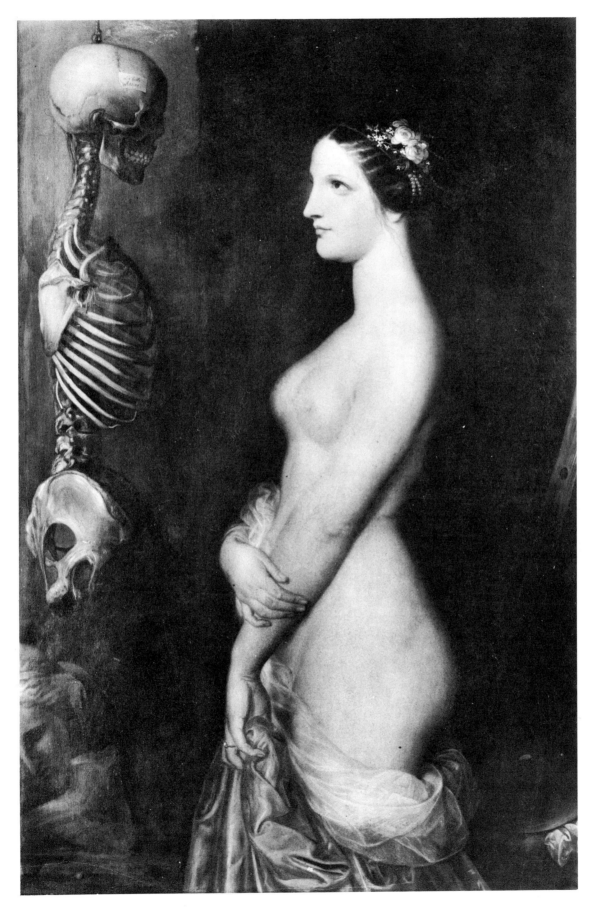

212

213

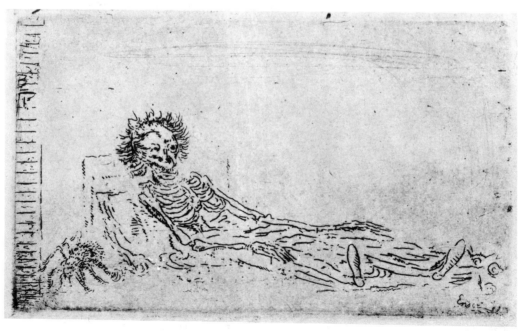

214

216

217

219

220

221

222

223

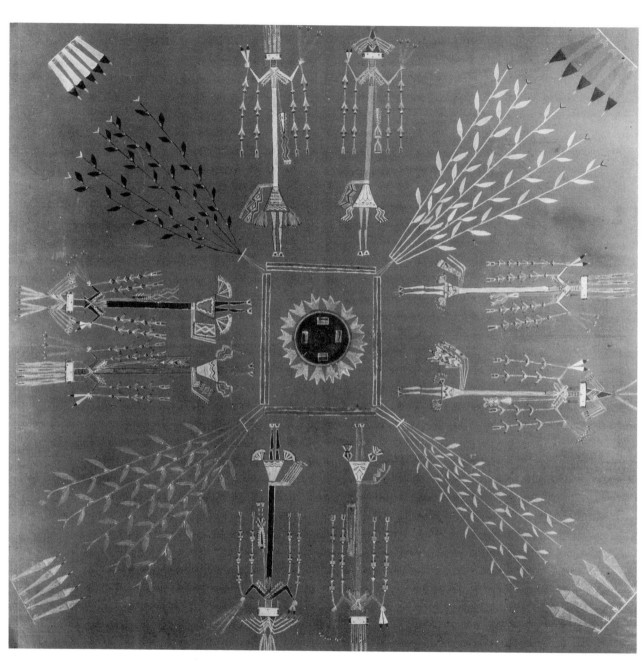

224

225

226

227

228

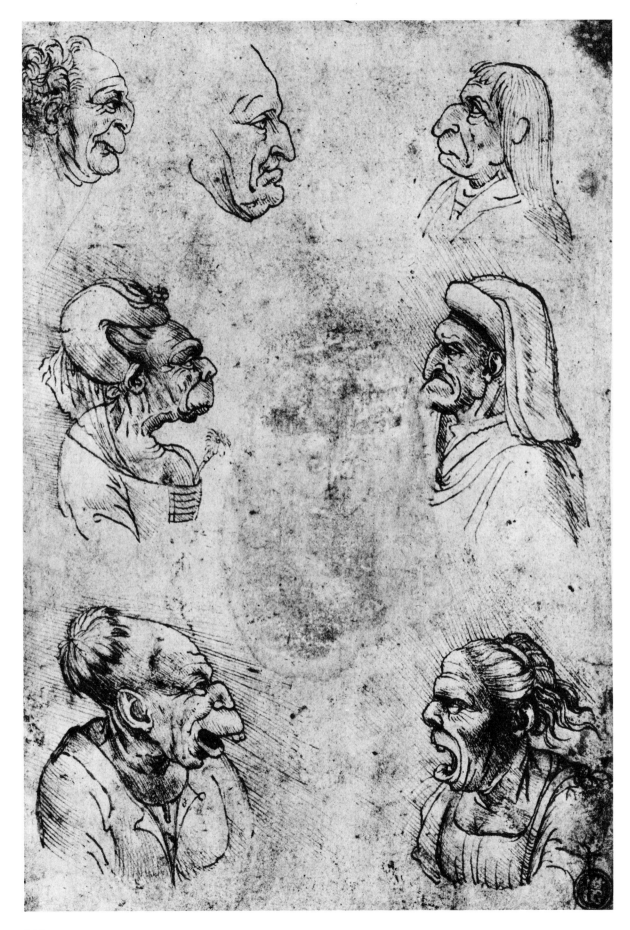

229

232

233

234

235

236

G.M. Mitelli I.e F.

C

Dal C Spronarti à la Costanza io sento,
E pero s'a lo studio utile è tanto,
Vna lettera sol uale per Cento.

G M Mitelli, I e F.

N

L'Enne amonisce ogni Pittor, che tale
Deue à gl'occhi mostrarsi ogni pittura,
Quale à gl'occhi si mostra il Naturale.

240

241

242

243

244

245

246

247

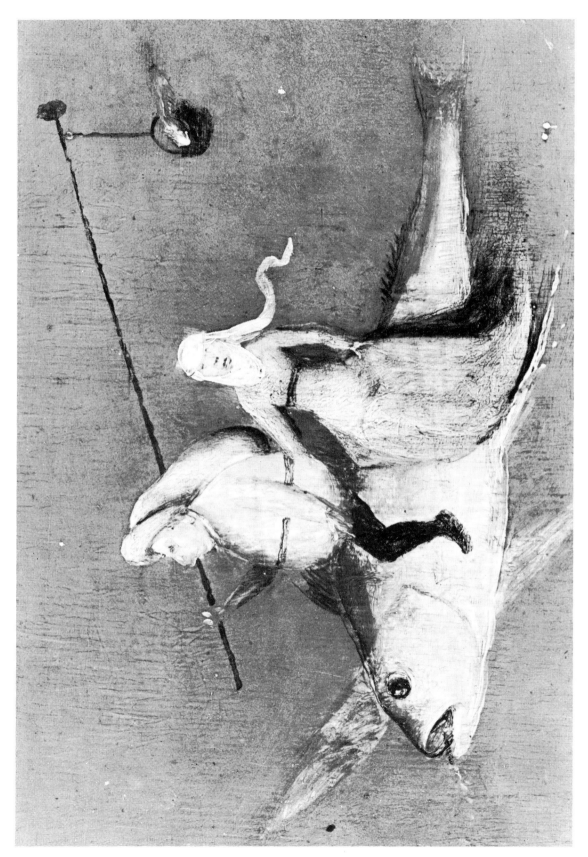

253

256

Quid modo diuitiæ, quid suluti vasta metalli
Congeries, nummis arca referta nouis,
Illecebres inter tantas, atq, agmina furum,
Iudicium cunctis efferis vnicus eris,
Præda facit furem, feruens mala cuncta ministrat
Impetus, et spolijs apta rapina feris.

Aux quatre Vents.

P. Bruegel inuen

Wel aen Ghy Spaerpotten, Tonnen, en Kisten,
Al sietmen v oog ander, willet niet Bedrouen.
Daerom vaert wij den haec die ons noyt en mist,
Mast soluic wel achte om ons te verdouen.
Maer men souwer niet kijæn, waerder niet te roouen.

Tis al om gelt en goet, dit stridenen twisten.

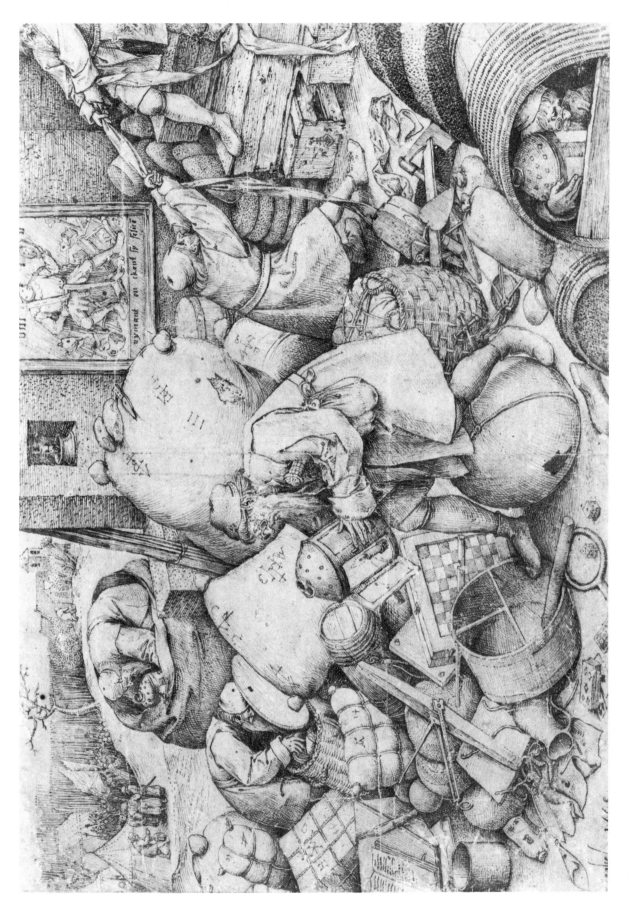

260

261

262

263

264

269

270

TAIL PIECE.

N°100

FINIS.

The Worlds End

A Nature Bankrupt

Design'd and Engrav'd by Wm Hogarth.

Publish'd according to Act of Parliam.^t March 3^d 1764.

THE BATHOS,
or Manner of Sinking, in Sublime Paintings,
inscribed to the Dealers in Dark Pictures.

271

Some of the Principal Inhabitants of y MOON, *as they Were Perfectly Discover'd by a Telescope brought to y* Greatest Perfection since y* last Eclipse, Exactly Engraved from the Objects, whereby y* Curious may Guess at their Religion, Manners, &c.*

Tab. I.

275

277

278

279

280

281

282

283

284

285

La sience positiviste et progresiste monte sur le rinoceros du Materialisme, le quel et constamment travessé par quelques "corpuscules irrationels". S. Dali. 1951

288

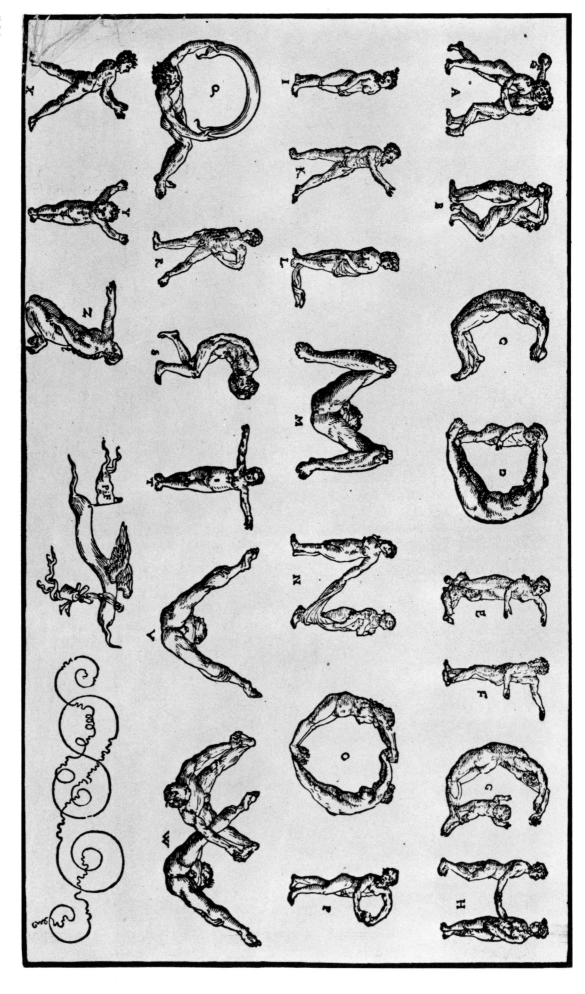

291

292

295

296

298

Selected Bibliography

ADELINE, J., *Les Sculptures grotesques et symboliques* (Rouen, 1879)

ANONYMOUS, "Exposition de masques et objets esquimaux de la collection de Charles Ratton" (*Cahiers d'Art 10*, 1935)

ANTAL, F., *Florentine Painting and its Social Background* (London, 1947)

Arts Plastiques, Les, 11-12, issue devoted to Bosch and Brueghel (Brussels, 1948)

BACHOFEN, J. J., *Das Mutterrecht* (Stuttgart, 1897)

BALDASS, L. von, *Hieronymus Bosch* (Vienna, 1944)

BALTRUSAITIS, J., *Le moyen âge fantastique* (Paris, 1955)

     Anamorphoses (Paris, 1956)

     Aberrations (Paris, 1957)

BARR, A. H., Jr. (ed.), *Fantastic Art, Dada, Surrealism* (New York, 1936)

BAUDELAIRE, CHARLES, *Curiosités esthétiques* (Paris, 1923)

BELL, C., *The Religion of Tibet* (Oxford, 1928)

BENDA, W. T., "Masks" (*Magazine of Art*, April 1946)

BERNHEIMER, R., *Wild Men in the Middle Ages* (Cambridge, Mass., 1952)

BLOOMFIELD, M. W., *The Seven Deadly Sins* (Lansing, Mich., 1952)

BORN, W., "Art of the Insane" (CIBA Symposia, January 1947)

    "The Dream in Art" (CIBA Symposia, September-October 1948)

    "Monsters in Art" (CIBA Symposia, August-September 1947)

    "Der Traum in der Graphik des Odilon Redon" (*Die Graphischen Künste*, 1929)

BOSCHÈRE, J. de, *Jerôme Bosch et le fantastique*, (Paris 1962)

BREDT, E. W., *Sittliche oder unsittliche Kunst?* (Munich, 1911)

    Hässliche Kunst (Munich, 1913)

BRETON, A., *L'Art magique* (Paris, 1957)

BRIDAHAM, L. B., *Gargoyles, Chimeras, and the Grotesque in French Gothic Sculpture* (New York, 1931)

BRION, M., "Le Singe de Dieu: Hieronymus Bosch" (*La Renaissance*, January 1939)

    Art fantastique (Paris, 1961)

BROWN, R., *The Unicorn* (London, 1913)

BRUNO DE JESUS-MARIE, *Satan* (New York, 1952)

BUHLER, W., *Kupferstichalphabet des Meisters E. S.* (Strassburg, 1934)

BUTLER, E. M., *The Myth of the Magus* (Cambridge, Mass., 1948)

CAMMELL, C. R., "Grotesque in Italian Art" (*The Connoisseur*, January 1935)

CAMPBELL, J., *The Hero with a Thousand Faces* (New York, 1949)

CARRIERI, P., *Fantàsia degli Italiani* (Milan, 1939)

CARUS, P., *History of the Devil and the Idea of Evil* (London, 1900)

CASTELLI, E., *Il demoniaco nell'arte* (Milan, 1952)

CASTIGLIONI, A., *Adventures of the Mind* (New York, 1946)

CHARCOT, J.-M., and RICHER, P., *Les Demoniâques dans l'art* (Paris, 1887)

    Les Difformes et les malades dans l'art (Paris, 1889)

CHASTEL, A., "La Tentation de Saint Antoine; ou Le Songe du mélancholique" (*Gazette des Beaux Arts*, April 1936)

CLARK, J. M., "The Dance of Death in the Middle Ages and the Renaissance" (*Burlington Magazine*, July 1951)

CLARK, KENNETH, "The Bizarie of Giovan Batista Braccelli" (*Print-collectors Quarterly*, October 1929)

CLARK, W. E., *Two Lamaistic Pantheons* (Cambridge, Mass., 1937)

CLOUZOT, H., and LEVEL, A., "L'Art fétiche africain" (*Revue de l'Art Ancient et Moderne*, June 1931)

DALL, W. H., *On Masks, Tabrets & Certain Aboriginal Customs* (Washington, D.C., 1884)

DANIEL, HOWARD, *Hieronymus Bosch* (New York, 1947)

    The World of Jacques Callot (New York, 1949)

DAVIS, H. M., "Fantasy" (*Metropolitan Museum of Art Bulletin*, June 1943)

DODGSON, C., "The Macabre in Two Centuries" (*Print-collectors Quarterly*, April 1929)

DUTHUIT, G., "Représentations de la mort" (*Cahiers d'Art* 4, 1939)

EMERSON, RALPH WALDO, "Demonology" (*Lectures and Biographical Sketches*, Boston, 1883)

ERICH, O. A., *Die Darstellung des Teufels in der christlichen Kunst* (Berlin, 1931)

EXHIBITION CATALOGUES

    Exhibition arranged by Fogg Art Museum on "The Tragic & The Grotesque Expressed by Masks & Clowns" (Cambridge, Mass., March 1935)

    Exhibition arranged by Pierpont Morgan Library on "The Animal Kingdom" (New York, 1940)

    Exhibition organized by the City of Rome, "Mostra del Demoniaco nell'arte" (Rome, 1952)

Exhibition arranged by Stedelijk Museum on "de duivel in de beeldende kunst" (Amsterdam, 1952)

Exhibition arranged by the Belgian Ministry of Education on "Art Fantastique" (Ostende, 1953)

Exhibition arranged by the City of Bordeaux on "Bosch, Goya et le fantastique" (Bordeaux, 1957)

Exhibition organized by Museum of Modern Art in collaboration with Art Institute of Chicago on "Redon, Moreau, and Bresdin" (New York, 1962)

Exhibition arranged by Royal Academy on "Goya and his Times" (London, 1963)

Exhibition arranged by British Museum of Goya Etchings and Lithographs (London, 1963)

FALKE, O. von, "Reiteraquamanilien: die Jägergruppe" (*Pantheon*, September 1929)

FELS, F., "Angel of the Bizarre; Representations of Death" (*Formes*, February 1930)

FENTON, E., "A Solitary Nomad in Paris" (*Metropolitan Museum of Art Bulletin*, January 1953)

FIERENS, P., *Le Fantastique dans l'art flamand* (Brussels, 1947)

FLOGEL-BAUER, K. F., *Geschichte des Grotesk-Komischen* (Munich, 1914)

FOCILLON, H. J. "The Fantastic in Mediaeval Art" (*Magazine of Art*, January 1940)

FRAENGER, WILHELM, *Der Bauern-Bruegel und das deutsche Sprichwort* (Zurich, 1923)

    The Millennium of Hieronymus Bosch (Chicago, 1952)

FRAZER, J. G., *The Golden Bough* (London, 1951)

FROMM, ERICH, *Psychoanalysis & Religion* (New Haven, 1950)

    The Forgotten Language (New York, 1951)

FUCHS, E., *Die Karikatur der europäischen Völker* (Munich, 1921)

    Geschichte der erotischen Kunst (Munich, 1912)

    Sittengeschichte (Munich, 1909)

GALLOP, R., "Masks of Indian Mexico" (*Apollo*, August 1938)

GANZ, PAUL, *The Drawings of Henry Fuseli* (New York, 1949)

GORI, GINO, *Il grottesco nell'arte e nella litteratura* (Rome, 1926)

GORDON, ANTOINETTE K., *Tibetan Religious Art* (New York, 1952)

    Iconography of Tibetan Lamaism (New York, 1929)

GOSSART, M. G., *La Peinture de diableries à la fin du moyen âge* (Lille, 1907)

GOULD, C., *Mythical Monsters* (London, 1886)

GRADMAN, E., *Phantastik und Komik* (Bern, 1958)

GRAF, ARTURO, *The Story of the Devil* (New York, 1931)

GRILLOT, GIVRY de, *Witchcraft, Magic and Alchemy* (New York, 1931)

GRÜNWEDEL, A., *Mythologie des Buddhismus in Tibet und der Mongolei* (Leipzig, 1900)

GUBERNATIS, ANGELO de, *Zoological Mythology* (London, 1872)

GUERRY, L., "Le Thème du triomphe de la mort dans la peinture italienne" (*Burlington Magazine*, July 1951)

GUNTHER, E., and INVERARITY, R. B., "Movable Masks and Figures of the North West Pacific Coast Indians" (*Design*, February 1942)

GUY, H. A., *The New Testament Doctrine of the Last Things* (Oxford, 1948)

HALL, H. U., "West African Masks" (*The Connoisseur*, June 1934)

HASTINGS, G. J. (ed.), *Encyclopedia of Religion and Ethics* (New York, 1951)

HAUSER, ARNOLD, *The Social History of Art* (New York, 1951)

HEILBRONNER, P., "Grotesque Art" (*Apollo*, November 1938)

HENDERSON, S. M. K., "African Masks and Sculpture" (*Glasgow Art Review 2*, 1946)

HOFFMAN, W., *Caricature from Leonardo to Picasso* (London, 1957)

HOLE, CHRISTINA, *Witchcraft in England* (New York, 1947)

HUXLEY, A., "Death and Baroque" (*Horizon*, April 1949)

IVANOFF, N., "Il grottesco nella pintura veneziana del seicento: Pietro il Vecchio" (*Emporium*, April 1944)

IVINS, W. M., Jr., "A Brueghel Exhibition in the Print Galleries" (*Metropolitan Museum of Art Bulletin*, March 1943)

JOHNSON, A. F., *Decorative Initial Letters* (London, 1931)

JUNG, C. G., *Psychology and Alchemy* (New York, 1953)

KAYSER, W., *Das Groteske* (Oldenbourg, 1958)

KITTREDGE, G. L., *Witchcraft in Old and New England* (Cambridge, Mass., 1929)

KLINGENDER, F. D., "Grotesque Ornament in Mediaeval Art" (*The Connoisseur*, November 1928)
  Goya in the Democratic Tradition (London, 1948)

KOZAKY, STEPHAN, *Geschichte der Totentänze* (Budapest, 1944)

KRIS, ERNST, *Psychoanalytic Explorations in Art* (New York, 1952)

KUBLER, G., "Cycle of Life and Death in Metropolitan Aztec Sculpture" (*Gazette des Beaux Arts*, May 1943)

KUP, K., "Prints: Artists' Impressions and Recordings of the Horrors and Miseries of War" (*American Artist*, January 1947)

LANGTON, E., *Satan—A Portrait* (London, 1945)

LAWLOR, H. C., "The Grotesque in Ancient Irish Sculpture" (*Formes*, June 1930)

LEGRAND, F. C., and SLUYS, F., *Arcimboldo et les Arcimboldesques* (Paris, 1955)

LEHNER, E., *Symbols, Signs and Signets* (Cleveland, 1950)
  Alphabets and Ornaments (Cleveland, 1952)

LEVRON, JACQUES, *Le Diable dans l'art* (Paris, 1935)

LEY, WILLY, *The Lungfish, the Dodo and the Unicorn* (New York, 1948)

LINTON, RALPH, and WINGERT, PAUL S., *The Art of the South Seas* (New York, 1946)

LÓPEZ-REY, J., *Goya's Caprichos* (Princeton, 1953)

LUM, PETER, *Fabulous Beasts* (New York, 1951)

LYNCH, B., *A History of Caricature* (London, 1927)

MACGOWAN, K., and ROSSE, H., *Masks and Demons* (New York, 1923)

MAETERLINCK, L., *Le Genre satirique dans la peinture flamande* (Brussels, 1907)
  Le Genre satirique dans la sculpture flamande (Paris, 1910)

MÂLE, E., *L'Art religieux du XIIe siècle en France* (Paris, 1924)

MALRAUX, ANDRÉ, *The Psychology of Art* (New York, 1949)

MARCHAND, GUYOT, *Dance of Death*, facsimile of 1490 edition (Washington, 1945)

MAUNDE-THOMPSON, G. E., "The Grotesque and the Humorous in Illuminations of the Middle Ages" (*Bibliographica II*, 1896)

MEAD, M., *Masks and Men* (Exhibition at American Museum of Natural History, New York, 1946)

MESPOULET, W., *Creators of Wonderland* (New York, 1934)

MICHEL, E., "Peter Huys au Musée du Louvre; Tentation de Saint Antoine" (*Gazette des Beaux Arts*, November 1935)

MICHEL, W., *Das Teuflische und Groteske in der Kunst* (Munich, 1911)

MICHELET, G., *Satanism and Witchcraft* (New York, 1946)

MOUSSON-LANAUZE, *Die Entwicklung der Heilkunde vom Empirismus zur Wissenschaft* (Paris, 1913)

MUHLE, W. H. v.d., *Die Darstellung des Jüngsten Gerichts an den romanischen und gothischen Kirchenportalen Frankreichs* (Leipzig, 1911)

MURRAY, M. A., *The Witch-Cult in Western Europe* (New York, 1921)
    The God of the Witches (New York, 1952)

NICOLAY, F., *Histoire sanglante de l'humanité* (Paris, 1909)

PACHTER, H. M., *Magic into Science—The Story of Paracelsus* (New York, 1951)

PANOFSKY, E., *Albrecht Dürer* (Princeton, 1944)
    Studies in Iconology (New York, 1939)

PERUGINI, M., "The Eccentric in Art" (*English Illustrated Magazine*, September 1905)

PHILLIPS, J. G., "Carved Stalls of the High Renaissance: Triumph in the Grotesque" (*Metropolitan Museum of Art Bulletin*, January 1941)

PORADA, EDITH, *Mesopotamian Art in Cylinder Seals of the Pierpont Morgan Library* (New York, 1947)

POUSETTE-DANT, N., "Distortion, Sweetness and the Grotesque" (*Prints*, April 1936)

PRAZ, MARIO, *Studies in 17th Century Imagery* (London, 1939)
    The Romantic Agony (London, 1951) ˙

RABELAIS, FRANÇOIS, *Les Songes drolatiques de Pantagruel*, facsimile of 1564 edition (Geneva, 1868)

REVILLE, A., *Histoire du diable* (Paris, 1904)

RIESMAN, DAVID, *The Lonely Crowd* (New Haven, 1950)

ROES, A., "Representation of the Chimaera" (*Journal of Hellenic Studies* 54, 1934)

ROGER-MARX, C., "Les Tentations de Saint Antoine" (*Gazette des Beaux Arts*, November 1936)

ROY, C., *Arts fantastiques* (Paris, 1960)

SAILER, A., "Heinrich Kley" (*International Advertising Art*, March 1939)

SAINT-EDMÉ, B., *Dictionnaire de la pénalité* (Paris, 1824–1828)

SAKISIAN, A., "Some Sino-Persian Monsters" (*Burlington Magazine*, February 1937)

SALOMON, R., *Opinions de Canistris* (London, 1936)

SCHARF, R., "Die Gestalt des Satans im Alten Testament" in C. G. Jung (ed.), *Symbolik des Geistes* (Zurich, 1947)

SEGY, L., *African Sculpture Speaks* (New York, 1952)

SELIGMAN, C., *A Mirror for Magic* (New York, 1947)

SERGEANT, P. W., *Witches and Warlocks* (London, 1936)

SEZNEC, J., "Temptation of St. Anthony in Art" (*Magazine of Art*, March 1947)

SHEPARD, O., *The Lore of the Unicorn* (New York, 1930)

SIREN, O., "Winged Chimaeras in Early Chinese Art" (*Eastern Art*, October 1928)

SITWELL, S., *Dance of the Quick and the Dead* (London, 1936)

SOLIER, R. de, *L'Art fantastique* (Paris, 1961)

SPINDEN, H. J., "African Masks and Fetishes" (*Brooklyn Museum Quarterly*, October 1935)
    Masks, Barbaric and Civilized (New York, 1939)

SPRENGER, JACOB, and KRAMER, HEINRICH, *Malleus Maleficarum* (London, 1948)

SUMMERS, MONTAGUE, *The History of Witchcraft and Demonology* (London, 1926)

SWAUGER, J. L., "Masks of the World" (*Carnegie Magazine*, December 1948)

TANNENBAUM, L., "James Ensor, Prophet of Modern Fantastic Art" (*Magazine of Art*, November 1943)

TAYLOR, F. H., "The Triumph of Decomposition" (*Parnassus*, April 1932)

TERVARENT, G. de, "Instances of Flemish Influence in Italian Art: in Monsters Raphael's Dream by M. Raimondi and Sleeping Woman and Somnus by the School of Dosso" (*Burlington Magazine*, December 1944)

TODD, RUTHVEN, *Tracks in the Snow* (New York, 1947)

TOLNAY, C. DE., *Hieronymus Bosch* (Basel, 1937)

   The Drawings of Peter Brueghel (London, 1952)

UGLOFF, L., "Drawings by Jacques Callot for the Temptation of Saint Anthony" (*Burlington Magazine*, November 1935)

UNDERWOOD, L., *Masks of West Africa* (London, 1948)

VALTON, E., *Les Monstres dans l'art* (Paris, 1905)

VAN MARLE, R., *Iconographie de l'art profane* (The Hague, 1932)

VAN MOÉ, E. A., *The Decorated Letter from the VIII to the XII Century* (Paris, 1950)

VAN PUYVELDE, L., *The Dulle Griet of Pieter Brueghel the Elder* (London, 1946)

VILLENEUVE, R., *Le Diable dans l'art* (Paris, 1957)

VINYCOMB, J., *Fictitious and Symbolic Creatures in Art* (London, 1906)

VOSS, GEORGE, *Das Jüngste Gericht in der bildenden Kunst des frühen Mittelalters* (Leipzig, 1884)

WEBER, F. P., *Aspects of Death and Correlated Aspects of Life in Art, Epigrams and Poetry* (London, 1918)

WEIGERT, R. A., "Grotesques" (*Art et Decoration 17*, 1950)

WESCHER, PAUL, "The Idea in Giuseppe Arcimboldo's Art" (*Magazine of Art*, January 1950)

WESSELY, J. E., *Die Gestalten des Todes und des Teufels in der deutschen Kunst* (Leipzig, 1876)

WIER, J., *Histoires, disputes et discours des illusions et impostures des diables, des magiciens infames, sorcières et empoisonneurs* (Paris, 1885)

WIERTZ, ANTOINE, *Oeuvres complètes* (Brussels, 1868)

WIGHT, F. S., "Masks and Symbols in Ensor" (*Magazine of Art*, November 1951)

WILSON, H., "Fantastic Designs by Tibetan Folk" (*Design*, March 1934)

   "Images Carved in Yak Butter and Paper Masks" (*Design*, March 1952)

WISSLER, CLARK, *Masks* (New York, 1946)

WITTKOWER, R., "Marvels of the East—A Study in the History of Monsters" (*Journal of the Warburg and Courtauld Institutes 5*, 1942)

WRIGHT, T., *History of Caricature and Grotesque in Literature and Art* (London, 1865)